A PRACTICAL GUIDE TO MINDFULNESS

This edition published in the UK
in 2018 by Icon Books Ltd,
Omnibus Business Centre,
39–41 North Road,
London N7 9DP
email: info@iconbooks.com
www.iconbooks.com

First published in the UK
in 2012 by Icon Books

Sold in the UK, Europe and Asia
by Faber & Faber Ltd,
Bloomsbury House,
74–77 Great Russell Street,
London WC1B 3DA
or their agents

Distributed in South Africa
by Jonathan Ball,
Office B4, The District,
41 Sir Lowry Road,
Woodstock 7925

Distributed in Australia and
New Zealand
by Allen & Unwin Pty Ltd,
PO Box 8500,
83 Alexander Street,
Crows Nest,
NSW 2065

Distributed in Canada
by Publishers Group Canada,
76 Stafford Street, Unit 300,
Toronto,
Ontario M6J 2S1

Distributed in the USA
by Publishers Group West,
1700 Fourth Street,
Berkeley, CA 94710

ISBN: 978-178578-383-8

About the author

Tessa Watt teaches mindfulness and is co-director of Being Mindful, which offers mindfulness training for the public and in workplaces. In her earlier career she was a research fellow in history at Cambridge University, and then for many years a senior producer in BBC Radio and Music.

Tessa has been practising meditation for over 25 years and is a senior teacher at the London Shambhala Meditation Centre. She did her mindfulness teacher training with the Centre for Mindfulness Research and Practice at Bangor University, and now teaches at SOAS, University of London. Tessa is a co-presenter of Be Mindful Online, the Mental Health Foundation's online mindfulness course, and author of *Mindful London*. She teaches and runs the mindfulness programme in the UK's Houses of Parliament and has been working with the All Party Parliamentary Group for Mindfulness to increase awareness of how mindfulness can benefit society.

Author's note

It's important to note that there is much frequently used teaching and research employed in mindfulness. Where I know the source I have been sure to reference it, but my apologies here to the originators of any material if I have overlooked them.

Contents

1. Introduction

Mindfulness is one of the oldest and most basic skills known to mankind. In its essence, it's as simple as rediscovering the taste of fresh water or the vastness of the sky. It is learning, or re-learning, how to be present, how to be in *this* moment. It can be like stepping out of a grey flat screen mode into a world which is vivid and three-dimensional.

Mindfulness means becoming more aware of what's going on – right here, right now. We can appreciate our lives, instead of rushing through them, always trying to get somewhere else. Being mindful can also help us to be less swept away by our powerful, habitual currents of thought and emotion, which can manifest as stress, depression, negative thinking, anxiety, anger, resentment or self-doubt.

Training in mindfulness

Mindfulness itself is a way of *being* – a capacity for moment-by-moment awareness – which doesn't belong to any one culture or tradition. But we find that this skill, part of our birthright, has somehow been lost to us; perhaps increasingly so in our speedy 21st-century world. The good news is that we can train ourselves in mindfulness, just as we exercise to keep our bodies healthy.

Mindfulness is about teaching yourself to be more:

• Aware – of your body, your mind and the environment

- Present – in this moment; right here, right now
- Focused – more able to make choices about where you place your attention
- Embodied – being *in* your body; bringing your mind and your body into synch
- Accepting – of yourself and other people.

Practice

Mindfulness training draws on the ancient traditions of meditation and yoga, often incorporating insights from modern medicine and psychotherapy. It involves setting aside time for 'practice' – time when you can literally practise being mindful by bringing your mind back, again and again, to a particular object of attention.

In mindfulness practice you may use one or more of these as your focus:

- Your breath – the physical sensations of breathing
- Your body – in stillness or in movement
- Your senses – such as hearing, seeing and tasting
- Your thoughts – which may include your emotions
- Your experience – whatever arises in your awareness in this moment, including any of the above.

As well as making space for formal meditation, you can bring mindfulness into your life throughout the day. You can use informal practices to help you do this – washing the dishes mindfully, perhaps, or taking a short 'breathing space'. With practice, the mindful approach will slowly seep into your being and you may find yourself naturally being more present and aware in your daily life.

 Mindfulness practice can be:

- Formal – such as sitting meditation using the breath as a focus
- Informal – such as making a cup of tea with awareness.

History

The practice of mindfulness goes back thousands of years. Many spiritual traditions have encouraged presence in the moment as a way to be in touch with our inner selves, or the divine. Buddhism has made mindfulness a core part of its teachings, more so than any other tradition. Buddhist thinkers have taken great interest over the centuries in the way the human mind works, developing methods of training the mind to be more present, focused and aware. The practical techniques used in current mindfulness training come largely from the Buddhist tradition of meditation, along with elements drawn from the more body-oriented Indian discipline of hatha yoga.

Since the 1960s, the political situation in Asian countries like Vietnam and Tibet has sent Buddhist teachers into exile in the West, where they've taken up the challenge of teaching new audiences. Meditation practices which were traditionally done by monks in a forest or monastery have been adapted for busy Westerners with jobs and families. Influential Buddhist teachers have included the Japanese Zen teacher Shunryu Suzuki, the Vietnamese monk Thich Nhat Hanh, the visionary Tibetan Chögyam Trungpa, and of course the well known Dalai Lama, spiritual leader of Tibet.

But you don't have to be religious, become a Buddhist or believe anything particular to practise mindfulness. Since the 1970s, mindfulness training in the West has developed into structured, secular courses which are increasingly accessible. Mindfulness has spread like wildfire in the public consciousness. In 1979 the American Jon Kabat Zinn created an eight-week course at the University of Massachusetts Medical School to help people with difficult conditions such as chronic pain, AIDS and cancer. Without being able to 'cure' them, he discovered that meditation could help them relate to their stress and suffering In a different way. This course of 'Mindfulness-Based Stress Reduction' (MBSR), is now used around the world; not only for people with illness, but for many thousands of participants simply wanting to find a way to deal with the normal daily difficulties of life, and to enjoy life more fully.

In the 1990s, mindfulness took its next quantum leap into the world of mental health and psychotherapy when three leading clinical psychologists from the UK and Canada developed Mindfulness-Based Cognitive Therapy (MBCT) as a treatment for people with a history of recurrent depression. MBCT is very similar to MBSR, with more emphasis on how to work with the 'negative thinking' which can lead to depression. Mindfulness has begun to sweep through the profession of psychotherapy, leading to other new therapies like ACT (Acceptance and Commitment Therapy); and many therapists now offer it to their clients as part of their toolkit for mental health.

In this book we'll introduce many of the practices and ideas which are used in mindfulness courses like MBSR and MBCT. We'll also draw inspiration from great mindfulness teachers coming from the Buddhist tradition, who carry with them years of deep training in the practice of meditation.

There are some key terms that will come up again and again in this book. It's worth taking a moment to acquaint yourself with them now …

Meditation is used in this book to refer to a formal practice which helps us train the mind to be more aware and present.

Mindfulness is used to describe a more general approach of being aware of our experience in the present moment – without judging it – which the practice of meditation can help us to develop.

Mindfulness-Based Stress Reduction (MBSR) is an eight-week course that trains participants to be mindful and to relate better to stress, pain and other difficulties.

Mindfulness-Based Cognitive Therapy (MBCT) is similar to MBSR but with elements developed more specifically for people with a tendency to suffer from depression.

Science

The move of mindfulness into public awareness is thanks largely to an explosion of interest from the scientific and medical communities within the last few decades. Research has demonstrated the enormous benefits of mindfulness practice for our physical and mental health, with new studies out every month. Doctors and counsellors increasingly recommend mindfulness as an approach for patients with depression, stress and anxiety-related ailments. Mindfulness training is also being adopted in schools and workplaces, helping students and employees to be more focused and productive, and less reactive to stress.

Research shows the benefits of mindfulness in many areas:

- **Physical health** – mindfulness can help us to cope better with a range of conditions including chronic pain, heart disease and cancer. It's been shown to strengthen the immune system, improving our response to illnesses ranging from flu to psoriasis to HIV.

- **Mental health** – mindfulness is increasingly being used to help people with recurrent depression, addiction, anxiety-related ailments, and general stress. Mindfulness participants have shown reduced levels of the hormone cortisol which is an indicator of stress.

- **Clarity and focus** – mindfulness meditators perform better in tasks measuring attention and comprehension, working memory, and creative problem solving. As our working lives become overloaded with information and input, studies suggest mindfulness can improve clarity and decision making, and it is now included in many leadership trainings.

- **Wellbeing** – many participants in mindfulness training have reported greater enjoyment and appreciation of their lives, as well as other benefits like greater self-awareness, greater acceptance of their emotions and increased empathy for other people. Neuroscientists are now backing this up with studies showing that meditation can strengthen areas of the brain associated with happiness, wellbeing and compassion.

Myths and misconceptions

The kind of meditation we use in mindfulness training is not about going off into altered states, trying to get to some better place. It's not about sitting in the lotus position in flowing white robes on a turquoise beach, as the advertising posters would have it – pleasant though that might be!

You're not even trying to get calm and relaxed, or to become a 'better person'. You are befriending the person you already are, and the place where you are sitting, right now. If you do experience any sense of calm, it is not from stilling the stormy weather of life, but from learning to ride its chaotic energy.

Here are some wrong ideas you might have about mindfulness:

- It's about going into an altered state where the mind is completely empty of thoughts
- It's about becoming very calm and not feeling emotions
- You have to become a Buddhist or take up some other religion or cult
- Even if other people can do it, you won't be able to because your mind is too busy.

How to use this book

Mindfulness is about experience, not just words and concepts. To get the most from this book, you'll need to do more than read – you'll need to actually *do* the practices.

 • **Take your time.** See if you can resist the urge to rush through to the end and 'get somewhere' quickly. It's better to do the practices thoroughly, and repeat them a number of times, than to think you are 'advancing' by ticking off lots of different exercises.

- **Keep a notebook.** Some of the exercises ask you to write a few lines. You may also like to keep a note of interesting or challenging things which arise in your practice. Writing things down in one place can help you reflect on your own experience and give you a sense of the journey you are taking.

- **Be patient.** Mindfulness is not a quick fix! Don't worry if you don't feel much is happening – there may be more going on under the surface than you think.

---

2. What is mindfulness?

Waking up

Mindfulness begins with recognizing that our common experience is *not* very mindful – that we are sleepwalking through much of our daily lives, blind and crashing into things. We stumble from place to place caught in a whirl-wind of thoughts, missing what is in front of our noses.

Often the storm of thoughts is not pleasant to be caught up in. We ruminate over what someone said earlier, or what we should have said in reply, or what happened ten years ago, or what we have to do tomorrow. Our minds are exhausting – we may feel exhausted.

The mindful approach is to invite a gap in this endless stream of thoughts and emotions. We train ourselves to wake up; to open a door and let in some fresh air and space. We're not pushing away our experience – quite the opposite. We're allowing ourselves to be present to the energy of our experience, right here, right now. We discover the possibility of waking up to how things are in each moment.

Awake and aware

Take a few minutes to become aware of your experience, right here, right now:

- Feel the weight and texture of the book in your hand.

- Feel the sense of your own body – your feet in contact with the floor, your buttocks on the chair; if you are sitting, feel your torso rising up, your head and shoulders, your arms and hands. Can you feel the movement of your breath somewhere in your body?

- Notice your environment – the space around you, any objects and people, any sounds and colours.

- Notice how you are feeling – are there any thoughts and emotions you are aware of? Are there any bodily sensations? You don't need to change anything, just notice. Spend a few moments opening your awareness to whatever is here in your body, mind and the environment.

Automatic pilot

In order to cultivate mindfulness, the first step is becoming aware of our usual tendency to sleepwalk through life. This mode is described as being on 'automatic pilot'. When we're on automatic pilot, we might eat a sandwich at our desk and reach the last crust without having ever actually tasted it. We might come home from work and find ourselves with the key in the door, having forgotten that we meant to stop to buy milk, and having completely missed seeing the blossom trees at the end of the road.

Our tendency to go onto automatic pilot can be particularly unhelpful when we start getting into negative trains of thought. Some small event may trigger us into feeling stressed or depressed, without us even realizing what is happening. Someone pushes in front of us in the queue, and subconsciously we set off on a train of thought about how no one respects us, and how the world is out to get us. Or perhaps a small task goes wrong at work, and before we know it we're convinced we can't finish our project and will lose our job. Most of us have some well-worn grooves into which our thoughts can easily begin to run. A few minutes later we find ourselves in a black mood, without even knowing how we got there.

Through mindfulness, we can recognize when we are on automatic pilot, and have a chance of stepping out into the freshness of the present moment. As we begin to pay attention to what is going on in our body, our mind and our environment, we can see how we get stuck on automatic pilot. By developing mindfulness, we can become more aware of the habits that make us unhappy or stressed, and start to make new choices. We can also become more present, more able to taste the richness of our world and all the little experiences which make up our lives.

A taste

One way to get a taste of mindfulness is to start quite literally with that – a practice of tasting. This is a good way to see what it's like when we bring our full awareness to a simple everyday experience.

Mindfulness courses around the world often start with tasting a raisin, a practice which has become traditional since Jon Kabat-Zinn included it in his pioneering clinic in the 1970s. If you don't have a raisin to hand, you can try this with whatever food you have available.

A taste of mindfulness

- Fetch yourself a couple of raisins, or if you don't have raisins you could use a segment of orange or other small piece of food.

- Look at it. Take the raisin or fruit in the palm of your hand. Imagine you've never seen anything like this before. Pick it up and take a good look at it, with your full attention. Notice the texture, the colour, the shape, the folds and hollows, the light shining on it. Take time to really see it and explore it with your eyes.

- Explore the raisin with your other senses. Give it a squish – perhaps even bring it up to your ear as you do so, to hear if it makes a sound. Notice what it smells like, and if you have any reaction to the smell, maybe in your mouth.

- Notice your thoughts. Whenever your mind wanders off, just be aware of this happening and aware of where your mind goes.

- Taste the food. First bring the object to your mouth, perhaps running it along the lips, noticing any reactions – maybe salivation. When you're ready, place it in

13

the mouth, not chewing yet. Pay attention to the sensations in your mouth, exploring it with your tongue. Finally prepare to chew the raisin, getting it into the right place – taking a bite into it, noticing the taste and texture in the mouth. Without swallowing yet, continue to chew, bringing your full attention to the taste of it.

- Swallow it: be aware first of your intention to swallow, and then actually swallowing the raisin – seeing if you can follow it as it moves down towards your stomach. And are there any after-effects – how do you feel after the exercise?

- And now, if you have a second raisin or piece of fruit, you might like to do the exercise again, slowly exploring this new object with each of your senses.

How was this exercise for you? Take a moment to reflect on what you've just done, and, if you'd like to, write your thoughts down.

Reflecting

Here are some responses that other people have had to this exercise:

- It tasted completely different to how I remembered; so much more flavour.
- My mind was really busy – I couldn't keep my focus on the exercise.

- I felt really irritated, and I wanted to go faster.
- I really noticed the texture of it, all the folds and colours. I was surprised that it made a noise when I squished it.
- It reminded me of Christmas and my grandmother's cakes.
- I don't like raisins so I could only think about how I didn't like it.

Was your experience different from the way you normally eat? Most of us would agree that it's rare to pay this much attention to what's happening when we're eating – to the flavours, textures, colours, and to the reactions going on in our body and mind. Normally we'd cram a handful of raisins in without thinking, or eat them in a bowl of muesli without noticing much about the taste of it.

This usual way of eating is a good example of being on automatic pilot. We go through many of our daily activities without being fully aware of what we're doing. By paying attention to our direct experience in this moment – whether it's a raisin, a cup of tea or a patch of bright sunshine, our lives can become more vivid. We can taste, smell and experience all the small moments that make up our lives, which we so often miss.

Paying attention
Jon Kabat-Zinn defines mindfulness in this way:

Mindfulness means paying attention in a particular way: on purpose, in the present moment and non-judgmentally.

We're always paying attention to *something*, but often not what we choose, as our mind jumps from one thing to another. Through practice we can pay attention:

- **On purpose**, by training ourselves to focus on an object of our choice, such as our left toes, or the movement of the breath

- **In the present moment**, being willing to let go of thinking about the past or the future, coming back to what is here now

- **Non-judgementally**, being kind to ourselves as we bring our minds back to the focus, over and over, developing gentleness and good humour. We don't judge our experience as 'good' or 'bad', we stay open to it all, just as it is.

A mindful meal

Eat a meal mindfully, in the same way that you ate the raisin (it doesn't have to be quite so slowly!). Put aside doing other activities at the same time, such as listening to the radio, talking or reading. Bring your awareness to the food as you are eating it; the tastes, the textures, the colours – and the act of eating itself.

- We live much of our lives in a mode which is not mindful, as though we are sleepwalking or on automatic pilot

- Mindfulness brings us out of automatic pilot into the present moment

- We can train ourselves to pay attention on purpose, in the present, and without judgement

- We can use small, simple experiences like tasting our food to begin to understand what it's like to be mindful.

Is this the right time for you?

Practising mindfulness is a brave thing to do. It means being willing to be alone with yourself – to be present with your own body and mind, without running away or distracting yourself with activities as most of us do. When we let ourselves be still, things we have buried or pushed down can come bubbling up to the surface – perhaps strong feelings or life events we haven't come to terms with. In mindfulness training, we don't generally get too involved in the content of these thoughts and emotions. Instead, as you'll see throughout this book, we let them come up, we notice with kindness how they affect us, and we let them move on.

If you are right in the midst of a very challenging or distressing life situation, such as a bereavement or a deep depression, this may not be the right time for you to start your practice of mindfulness. The emotions may feel too overwhelming for you to be present with them in the way that mindfulness encourages. At this point it may be best to seek professional support from your doctor or a psychotherapist, and continue your exploration of mindfulness when things are a bit more settled in your life. When your mind is more stable, you will be in a better position to learn and practise this new way of approaching things. Mindfulness will then be a skill for life which can help you cope better with difficult events when they arise in the future.

3. Why?

What are you doing here? Why are you reading this book instead of a novel or a newspaper? What has piqued your interest in mindfulness and what do you hope to get from it?

It's helpful to have an idea of our intention before we begin a journey. When things are challenging, we can remember our initial inspiration, and find the motivation to go forward. Your intention might be a bit vague – a feeling that something is missing, a general sense of longing, or a curiosity. That's fine. See if you can articulate something about it right now, before you are influenced by reading more about other people's intentions.

Intention
- Sit quietly for a few moments. Bring your awareness into your body. Spend a few moments feeling your feet on the floor, the weight of your body on the seat and your hands wherever they are resting. Feel your spine and head rising upwards.

- Ask yourself, 'Why am I here, reading this book? What do I hope to get from learning about mindfulness?' Notice what first comes into your mind.

- Sit with the question for a few moments. Let it settle in your mind, and see what arises in response. Is there anything deeper under the surface? Are there any half-formed thoughts or feelings that you can put into words?

- Write down your response here or in a notebook where you can find it again:

_____

_____

_____

_____

_____

Why mindfulness?
Now, have a look at some of the reasons other people choose to take up mindfulness practice. See if any of these motives resonate with you:

- To become more relaxed and calm
- To cope better with stress and anxiety
- To help prevent myself from getting into depression

- To have better concentration and focus
- To cope with chronic pain or illness
- To enjoy and appreciate my life more
- To handle strong emotions more successfully
- To have greater self-awareness and insight
- To be more accepting of myself and others
- To connect with a sense of meaning or something bigger than myself
- To have more sense of space in my life.

Every month new research papers are published on the use of mindfulness in coping with particular physical and mental health issues such as drug addiction, tinnitus or OCD. Other studies focus on specific groups of participants, such as parents, students or prisoners, while still others look at mindfulness in relation to general wellbeing. *The Mindful Manifesto*, by Ed Halliwell and Jonty Heaversedge, gives an inspiring overview of the evidence for mindfulness and its benefits. Here are some of the key areas where mindfulness has been shown to be helpful …

Stress
Researchers have been interested for some years in the effects of meditation on stress levels, but it was hard to test in a clinical setting. The Mindfulness-Based Stress Reduction course is a good subject for clinical research because of its standardized, replicable format. Numerous studies have now shown that MBSR does what it says on

the tin: it reduces stress and helps people cope with it more effectively.

Stress is a natural response of our bodies to threat. As part of our evolution we developed the 'fight or flight response', a state of hyper-arousal in which our body prepares us to fight an attacker or run away to safety. We're no longer often threatened by physical dangers like wild animals, but our nervous system kicks in with the same responses in reaction to modern stresses like work deadlines and traffic jams. We lose the ability to flick the off switch, and find ourselves in a perpetual state of raised heart rate, high blood pressure and pumping adrenaline.

Mindfulness practice has been shown to have a calming effect on the nervous system, helping to switch off the stress response and bring us back into balance. It also trains us to become more aware of stress signals in the body, giving us the chance to respond more effectively. We can take intelligent action rather than reacting blindly by losing our temper, drinking too much, overworking, or whatever else we tend to do.

Tessa (the author)

'I've always been quite a speedy person – walking quickly, talking quickly. I grew up with severe eczema which meant I was itchy all the time; literally uncomfortable in my own skin. In my twenties I moved from a quiet life in a university town to working as a trainee producer on live national radio. It was exciting but hugely stressful. My eczema got so bad that when I went on holiday in Corsica I couldn't even go swimming. I sat under a fig tree reading a 'teach yourself meditation' book that I had picked up at the airport. I started doing the practices, and I had a glimpse of feeling very different – a sense of coming back inside myself and being content where I was, sitting under that tree.

'Back in London I found a meditation centre, and began to do courses there, and to practise at home. It gave me some stillness in my stressful life, and my itchy skin also calmed down. But as time went on the mindfulness became something much wider and deeper. It seeped into every aspect of my life. I realized how often I was caught up in my repetitive thought patterns – planning and worrying – and that when I let them go there was a whole big world out there. It was a bit like that moment in *The Wizard of Oz*, when Dorothy steps out from black and white into glorious Technicolor.

'It's not that my thoughts and worries have gone away. But I know that at any moment, when I remember, I can drop them and wake up to a world which is much more vivid and spacious. This sense of greater space has also helped me to be less reactive. When a strong emotion like fear or anger starts to rise up in me, I can let myself feel the feelings and allow myself a bit of a gap, without always reacting blindly. If I go for any length of time without doing my mindfulness practice, I can notice the difference – how

my thoughts become more claustrophobic and how challenging situations feel a bit more stressful.'

Depression

In the 1990s, three clinical psychologists – Mark Williams,
John Teasdale and Zindel Segal – were developing a new
treatment for people with recurrent depression using
Cognitive Behavioural Therapy (CBT). They were inspired
by Jon Kabat-Zinn's MBSR clinic, and decided to include
mindfulness in their programme. What began as a course
in CBT which had bits of mindfulness tacked on, eventually became a course with mindfulness as its core, with
elements of CBT woven in. Mindfulness-Based Cognitive
Therapy (MBCT) has tested very favourably in trials compar-
ing it with other forms of treatment, and is now endorsed
in the UK by the National Institute for Health and Clinical
Excellence for use with people who've suffered more than
two episodes of depression.

If you're prone to depression, you probably have a tendency to 'ruminate' – to get caught up in spirals of obses-
sive thoughts which are hard to distinguish from facts.
Through mindfulness you can learn to stay grounded in the
body and to be less caught up in the mind. You can start to
see that your thoughts are not reality, and take a step back
from them. You can learn to see the early warning signs that
a spiral of low mood is starting, and so have a chance of
taking a different direction.

The best time to take up mindfulness is not when you are already in the midst of severe depression, but when things are on a somewhat more even keel, when you have the patience and stability to build up skills for your long-term mental health. If you think you may be suffering from depression but have not yet had any advice, it's important to consult your doctor. You may need some professional support such as psychotherapy or medication to help you back into a more healthy state, from which learning mindfulness can be of real benefit to you in the longer term.

Pain

When Jon Kabat-Zinn started teaching mindfulness at the University of Massachusetts medical school, many of the patients suffered from conditions causing them chronic pain. The aim of such patients learning mindfulness was not to remove the pain, but to teach them a new way of relating to it. Research showed that 65 per cent of patients who hadn't responded to conventional medical treatments were less troubled by pain after learning mindfulness. Neuroscientific research is now showing that meditation actually creates changes in areas of the brain which process and regulate pain, and this looks set to be a big area for continued study.

Marion

*Marion is a visual artist who has lupus, a con-
dition where the immune system attacks the
body causing damage in the joints, muscles and other
organs. After eight years of intense, erratic pain, she signed
up for a mindfulness course.*

I was at a state of desperation. I was at the stage where
I thought if the rest of my life is going to be like this I'm
not sure I can actually make it. I always thought meditation
sounded hippy-ish, not really for someone like me, but at
this point I thought 'I've got absolutely nothing to lose.'

I think the first thing I learnt from the mindfulness was
how much time I spent not experiencing what I was experiencing, but being in the past or future with it. Spending a
lot of time feeling very sad about what I'd lost, and project-
ing into the future with a lot of fear – 'Is this going to get
worse? Am I ever going to get well? Am I ever going to be
able to work again?' Mindfulness gave me a tiny bit of time
in each day when I was actually in the moment, in the now,
in a non-judgemental way.

Then during a meditation I tried going right up to the
edge of the pain. I'd done loads of pain management and
pain reduction techniques previously – but with the mindfulness it's not about managing it or reducing it, it's about
going up to it and saying, 'This is how it is in my body at
the moment.' It's absolutely counter-intuitive, but the way
it works is incredibly interesting.

The way I understand it is that pain happens in a lot of different places in the brain. There's the actual initial nerve sending out an impulse saying you're experiencing pain, and then there's a whole chain of other things that happen around the pain that are maybe to do with anxiety or fear or a whole wide range of emotions. By meditating with those emotions – allowing those emotions to actually be and coming up close to them – I've found that although my pain hasn't gone, my experience of the pain is very different. I would say that it's really dramatically changed my experience of illness.

Illness

Mindfulness is not a cure for illness, but it's been shown to improve the body's ability to cope with a variety of physical conditions. Stress can weaken the response of the immune system, while evidence suggests that mindfulness can strengthen it:

- A research team gave flu jabs to two groups of participants. The group which had trained in mindfulness had a stronger response to the vaccine, producing more antibodies.

- A group of women were offered MBSR after surgery from breast cancer. Their immune systems recovered more quickly than those of the women who were not practising mindfulness.

- Another study measured the effects of mindfulness on people with HIV. The group which had 8 weeks of mindfulness training maintained a constant level of CD4 T cells, which play a key role in coordinating the immune system. In the control group without mindfulness training, the cell count dropped over the same period.

Happiness and wellbeing

Mindfulness can help us cope better with stress, depression, illness and pain, but you don't have to be dealing with any of these specific challenges for it to be of value. It is a skill which can help you to live life more fully and wisely; to be more at ease with yourself and happier in your own skin. Here are some comments students have made after a course in mindfulness:

I learnt to slow down, to appreciate the moment, to breathe.

Dan

I have this small space developing in my life, one that is calm, a place that I can reach for in moments of stress and pain. So I've realized that peace is not something I need to wait for after I have finished my to-do list.

Rebecca

I learnt that I do have a wise and gentle part of myself. The practice helped me to rediscover it.

Alessia

I've begun to understand what 'being in the moment' actually means. It's not just a bumper sticker. Also, I've learnt not to be so hard on myself – or at least started.

Sarah

I've become more accepting of all the bits of me that make me human – sadness, anger, frustration, fear and so on.

Anna

I discovered there is a different way of viewing the world or situations – that sometimes just stopping and observing is the best thing to do. And that anyone can meditate – it's not some special place or state.

Alex

The experience of people who practise mindfulness is now being backed up by science. Within the past few years, neuroscientists have been using MRI technology to look at the brains of people who meditate. The results have been fascinating.

We now know that just as muscles can strengthen with exercise, the brain can strengthen in certain regions according to how we use it. For example, the brains of medical students involved in intense periods of study show changes in the areas important for memory, while jugglers' brains show increased connections in the regions which anticipate moving objects. And now a number of studies have shown that meditators have more activity and grey matter in areas of the brain associated with happiness, wellbeing and the ability to regulate emotion. Changes have been documented not only in seasoned meditators of many years, but also in participants with just eight weeks of mindfulness practice.

Reviewing your intention

Now that you've read more about some of the benefits of mindfulness, look again at what you wrote down as your intention. Is there anything you would like to add?

You may find you have one or two intentions which are quite specific – perhaps to become less stressed at work or to cope better with a difficult relationship. You may also have an intention or two which feel broader, or deeper – to feel more at ease or to enjoy life more.

Make any additions or changes you'd like to make, and keep your written intention where you can find it again later.

Journey without a goal

Although it's good to have a sense of where you'd like to be heading, this is not about programming your sat nav with a specific postcode and address, and expecting to arrive in 2 hours 45 minutes. Mindfulness helps us to open ourselves to a wider and fresher world of possibilities, and we may find that the journey takes us in unexpected directions. Your experience will be much richer if you can be open to the changes of landscape, and to revising your intentions as you go along.

It's also good to relax about monitoring your progress and expecting to see 'benefits' too obviously or quickly. Paradoxically, for mindfulness practice to be of any benefit we need to drop our constant judgement and stop looking for results. Mindfulness is not a quick fix – we are retraining habits that have been ingrained in us for years or even decades. Sometimes the practices bring internal shifts which are slow, subtle and not obvious to our conscious mind until further down the line. One of the hardest things to grasp is that mindfulness works not by looking for changes, but by becoming more accepting of who we are right now. So we cultivate an attitude of non-doing and non-striving, which is the opposite of what we are used to! We'll talk more about this in Chapter 8.

When participants finish an eight-week mindfulness course, one of the most frequent comments they make as a recommendation to others is, 'Just do it. Don't judge it, just do the practice.' You are welcome to decide at the end of the course, or the book, whether mindfulness is something you find of benefit and want to carry on with. Meanwhile, see if you can suspend your judgement and do the practices without worrying too much each time whether they are doing you any good.

Finally, of course, the journey is your own, and though this book can give you some direction, you have to do the travelling yourself. It's fine to read, but the more you actually practise the exercises, the more you'll get your own feel for the path of mindfulness and where it can take you.

It's good to have an idea of your intention in practising mindfulness. This will help give you the motivation to practise.

BUT

Keep an open mind. See if you can do the practices without constant judgement or looking for immediate benefits.

4. Space

Mindfulness can help us to create space within the rush and busyness of our lives. In fact we talk about 'creating' space but we don't actually have to *create* it – the space is already here, open and infinite. We're creating a gap, in which we can *allow* the space instead of constantly filling it up with our activity.

Being

What does it mean to be a human being? The mindful answer puts the emphasis on the word 'being'. We are human *beings*, but we have forgotten how to *be*. We have become human *doings*, trapped in a mode of always doing, acting, achieving and keeping busy. When we stop, even for a moment, it can feel frightening and unnatural. Activity and busyness have become our default mode.

In the mid-20th century when Eastern teachers started bringing the practice of meditation to the Western public, it went against the grain. Here was a practice which encouraged you to sit there, seemingly doing nothing. It appeared self-indulgent and navel-gazing. Early adopters were seen as part of the counter-culture, including literary and musical figures such as Jack Kerouac, Alan Ginsberg and Leonard Cohen.

Meditation has become much more mainstream since then, growing steadily in popularity as thousands of 'ordinary' people have tasted its benefits. When Jon Kabat-Zinn began teaching mindfulness at his Stress Reduction Clinic in the 70s, American truck-drivers and grandmothers found themselves sitting cross-legged in silence or twisting themselves into yoga postures: it felt 'un-American' as one participant put it. But it changed their lives. Patients on the edge of despair learned to stop struggling with their conditions, to re-inhabit their bodies, and to enjoy life again.

Mindfulness practice allows us time and space to be. It may be setting aside half an hour for the formal practice of meditation. Or it may be allowing a few seconds gap – a moment of pause.

It's not about spacing out, vegetating or going into an altered state, but *being* with awareness. Being aware of where we are and what is happening, right now. It doesn't mean we can't achieve things. In fact by training ourselves to shift regularly into this mode of *being*, it's more likely that our *doing* mode will be effective, focused and productive.

Being versus doing

The Western Christian tradition is often associated with the protestant work ethic; with 'doing' and being active. But the Bible contains passages in which Christ encourages his listeners not to worry about material provisions, and celebrates the value of being rather than always doing.

Consider the lilies of the field, how they grow;
They toil not, neither do they spin

Matthew 6:28

More recently, the value of taking time out for being has been encapsulated in bumper-sticker wisdom: 'Don't just do something, sit there!'

Pause

The space we create for mindfulness can come in all sizes. There are formal meditation sessions where you set aside time for practice – perhaps for 10, 20, 30 or more minutes a day. Many dedicated practitioners take part in longer retreat sessions lasting for a day, a week, a month, or even several years at a time, like the Englishwoman Tenzin Palmo who lived for 12 years in a Himalayan cave.

At the other end of the spectrum, mindfulness practice can be done in the blink of an eye. We can pause at any time in the busy stream of our day, taking a moment to notice where we are. When we find ourselves in fast-forward mode, we can press the pause button. Perhaps just for a few seconds, we can step out of automatic pilot and bring awareness to what's happening here and now in our body, our mind and the environment. Then, without making a big deal of it, we can carry on with our day.

The American Buddhist nun Pema Chödrön is a much-loved meditation teacher and writer. In recent years she has been emphasizing the practice of 'pausing' more and more in her teaching. As she writes in *Taking the Leap*, 'We can always connect with the openness of our minds. We can use our days to wake up rather than go back to sleep. Give this approach a try. Make a commitment to pausing throughout the day, and do that whenever you can.'

A pause

Stop reading. Take just a few seconds to notice whatever is right here, right now. Your body. Your thoughts and emotions. The environment around you. Any sights, sounds or smells.

Take a few mindful breaths, being aware of the movement of the breath in and out of your body.

Then carry on.

The practice of pausing is not meant to be a substitute for more formal meditation – the two go hand in hand. With meditation we make time to step out of our normal whirl-wind of activity and cultivate our ability to be present; to connect with a greater sense of spaciousness. Then, as we train our minds through meditation, we can also let this permeate our daily lives through small and frequent pauses throughout the day. When we become trapped in the claustrophobia of busy thoughts, we can open up to a bigger space, like puncturing holes in a dense cloud so that the sun can shine through.

Your pause button

Pick something that you can use as a trigger or reminder for your 'pause' practice. It could be:

- A sound you hear often in the day such as a phone, car alarm or siren

- A visual cue such as a sign or image on your computer or fridge

- An activity you do often such as washing your hands or sending a text message.

Make a decision that each time you hear or see or do this thing, you'll just pause for a few seconds, notice where you are and what's happening, take a few mindful breaths, and then move on.

Your pause button:

_____

_____

_____

_____

• Mindfulness creates space for 'being' rather than 'doing'

- If you allow time for being, it will help your doing to be more productive

- Set aside time for formal meditation practice – even 5 or 10 minutes a day is a good start

- You can also train yourself to create little spaces, pausing often throughout the day. Use a sound, visual cue or activity as a reminder.

5. Breath

Breathing is the most basic human function – to know we are breathing is to know we are alive. So, it's not surprising that mindfulness of breath has been practised for millennia.

Awareness of the breath is available to us in any moment. No special equipment is needed – our breath is always with us. Here is a movement which is going on 24 hours a day, most of the time without us noticing it. There is nothing especially mystical about it – we just practise bringing awareness to this most simple and universal activity.

When you bring awareness to your breath, it is *this* breath, in *this* moment – not last year's breath or tomorrow's breath. The breath is closely connected to the body, and also to the mind; it is a link or bridge between the two. When you tune in to your breathing, your body and mind are in synch – you are present. You can train yourself to use the breath as a haven, or an anchor: when you find you are caught up in a whirlwind of thoughts, you can let it go and come back to this natural process of breathing.

Mindfulness of breathing
You can do this practice for any length of time – for the first time you could try 5 minutes. Sit on an upright chair with your feet flat on the floor, or cross-legged on a firm cushion.

Taking your seat:
- Come into a posture which feels relaxed and awake, with a tall spine.
- Let your shoulders drop and your hands rest on your thighs.
- Close your eyes or keep them open with a downward gaze, whichever feels most comfortable.
- Feel the weight and gravity of your body. Notice the sensations where your buttocks connect with the chair or cushion, and where your feet or ankles make contact with the floor. Spend a few moments exploring these sensations.

Being with your breath:
- Bring your attention to the movement of your breath, wherever you feel it. There's no need to change the way you're breathing, or do anything special with the breath. Just let it be as it is.
- Tune in to the physical sensations of breathing – not *thinking* about the breath but *being* with it, allowing the breath to breathe itself. See if you can be with the breath all the way in and all the way out. You can imagine you are riding on the waves of your own breath if you find this helpful.

Bringing back your mind:
- You will find that your mind wanders off from the breath – that's not a problem. A mind naturally wanders. You

may find yourself daydreaming or worrying, replaying a conversation or running through a shopping list. Whenever you notice your mind has gone off, gently return your attention to the breath.

• If your mind wanders from the breath a hundred times, just bring it back a hundred times. See if you can escort your awareness back to the breath with kindness and good humour. This is the practice: not keeping the mind fixed in one place, but bringing the mind back, over and over. Use the breath as an anchor to bring you back to here and now, to this moment.

Take a moment to write down anything you noticed during your practice of mindful breathing (either here or in a notebook):

_____

_____

_____

_____

Is your breath boring?
In, out, in, out, in, out …

You may find your breath somewhat less entertaining than watching the TV or reading a newspaper. Of course if you were in a situation where you found yourself running out of air, unable to breathe, you would suddenly find your breath very interesting indeed!

In mindful breathing, it helps to cultivate a curiosity about your own breath. See if you can be inquisitive, bringing a fresh interest to the breath, as if you had never noticed it before. Here are some things you might like to investigate:

- **Breath in the nostrils** – can you notice the feeling of cool air going in, and warmer air going out?
- **Breath in the torso** – do you feel it moving in the upper chest, in the mid-torso or in the belly? See if you can follow your breath down into the belly, noticing how the walls of the abdomen expand like a balloon on the inhale, and relax back again on the exhale. It may help to put a hand on your belly, so that you can feel the rise and fall of the breath.
- **Qualities of the breath** – does your breath feel long or short? Shallow or deep? Rough or smooth? Can you feel the texture of it? Does it change or stay the same?
- **Inhale and exhale** – what's it like to follow the in-breath in, and then the out-breath out? What happens at the point where the inhale turns into the exhale, and the exhale to the inhale? Does the breath flow straight on, or is there a gap?
- **Breath dissolving** – what happens when the breath leaves your nose or mouth? Do you have a sense of

it dissolving and mixing with the space in front and around you? How far does it go? How does it feel as your breath flows out of the body – perhaps some sense of releasing and letting go?

Remember, you don't have to change anything or manipulate the breath, just be gently inquisitive about each breath – *this* breath, in *this* moment.

Mindfulness of breathing: being inquisitive
Repeat the mindful breathing exercise from page 39, but this time pick one or more aspects of the breath from the list we just ran through to focus on. Spend a few minutes really feeling the texture of the breath, or the sensations of the breath in the belly. Are there other things you can notice about your breath which are not on this list?

Is your mind busy?
'I can't meditate – my mind is too busy'. This is one of the most common first reactions to the mindful breathing exercise.

When you start to meditate, you may find it shocking how active your mind is. It flits from one thought to another, often without any obvious logic. It may feel like a monkey leaping from tree to tree. You may even think,

'I was looking for calm, but when I started to meditate my mind got busier!' It's more likely that your mind has been this busy all along, but only now are you creating the conditions for noticing the busyness.

In mindfulness we don't see thoughts as a 'problem' – we are not trying to get rid of thoughts to achieve an empty, blank state of mind. Having thoughts is part of who we are as creative, thinking beings. It can be hard to believe this when you start, but the practice of meditation is actually just this: noticing the thoughts, letting them go and bringing the mind back to the focus, again and again. Each time your mind wanders off, it's another opportunity to practise bringing it back.

Mindfulness is not about having a mind that is empty and blank. Your mind will have lots of thoughts, and that is okay!

Take your seat

The classic meditation posture you see in ancient sculptures is cross-legged on the floor, with the feet tucked up in the lotus position. After years of sitting in chairs and at desks, most of us don't bend that way anymore! That's not a problem – the seated mindfulness practices can be done on a chair, cross-legged on a cushion or kneeling if it's comfortable for you.

A chair:
- Choose a firm chair with an upright back.
- Sit with your feet flat on the floor or place something firm under your feet if they don't reach the floor.
- Ideally, let your spine be self-supporting, sitting away from the back of the chair or with the chair back lightly supporting you. If it's not comfortable, a cushion in the small of the back may help.

A cushion:
- If you have the chance, you can try sitting on a specially designed meditation cushion; they come in many shapes and sizes
- Your seat should be firm, not too squishy – try placing a cushion from your chair or sofa on top of large books such as phone books
- Your ankles can be crossed comfortably, resting on a blanket or mat. Your knees should be a bit lower than your hips. For many of us with stiff hips, this means we need to get our seat quite high up off the ground (perhaps 8–12 inches or more).

Kneeling:
- Some people find it comfortable to kneel, with a cushion under the buttocks and shins on either side of the cushion. You can also buy wooden meditation stools which are used in this kneeling position.

Posture

As a child, you may have been told to, 'Sit up straight!' As a result, you might even have a secret resistance to the idea of posture. But when we meditate in a sitting position, taking a good posture is the foundation of the practice. Our bodies and minds are connected – when the body slumps, the mind slumps. When the body is uplifted and awake, it encourages the mind to be this way too. Here are some tips for a good posture:

- **Have a firm base** – sit solidly on your seat, feeling the weight of your buttocks on the chair or cushion. Feel the contact of your feet flat on the floor; or the ankles or shins if you are cross-legged or kneeling.

- **Be alert** – your spine is tall, the crown of your head lifting towards the sky. You can imagine sitting like a mountain, or like a monarch on a throne – regal and present.

- **Be comfortable** – your posture is uplifted but not rigid. Let your shoulders relax, and your hands rest on your thighs. The front of the body can be soft and open. Let your jaw be loose, and perhaps tuck your chin slightly in. If your eyes are open, look downward a few feet in front of you, with a gaze which is soft and relaxed.

Is breathing difficult?

Some people find mindful breathing difficult because of problems with their breath. It may be a physical issue, or it may be that each time you focus on your breath you start to panic that you can't breathe properly. If this is you, don't worry; it may be good to focus on other mindfulness practices for now, especially bringing your awareness into your body and its sensations. You may find that as you feel more grounded and at home in your body, your breath also starts to feel more comfortable.

Your breath is available to you at any time as an anchor to bring you back into your body and into the present moment.

Mindfulness of breathing: through the week

Now that you've tried mindful breathing, see if you can practise it again during the week. You can set aside a few minutes for formal practice – 5 minutes, 10 minutes or whatever you can manage.

You can also bring your awareness to the breath at any time during your day, just noticing that you are breathing for a few breaths, and then moving on.

6. Brushing your teeth

Mindfulness practice is sometimes described as being a bit like brushing your teeth. It's something you can do every day as part of your basic mental hygiene. It's better to brush your teeth every day for 5 minutes, rather than for an hour on Sundays. In the same way, it's good to keep the connection with your mindfulness practice by doing a little each day, rather than saving it up for sporadic marathon sessions.

You can also use the act of brushing your teeth quite literally as a chance to practise mindfulness. Instead of mechanically going through the motions while you are busy thinking of other things, you can be aware of your tooth-brushing while you are doing it, tuning into the physical sensations and being aware of your environment. Awareness of a simple daily activity like this can help you bring yourself into the present moment, and offers a practice you can do even at the busiest of times.

Mindful tooth brushing

Next time you brush your teeth, see if you can do it mindfully:

- Be aware of putting the toothpaste on the brush, bringing the brush to your mouth, the actions of your hand,

sensations in your gums and mouth, the taste of the toothpaste.
- You can also be aware of your environment – any sounds, and objects in your vision, perhaps your face in the mirror.

You don't need to be too precious or self-conscious about it – or become a perfectionist tooth brusher (although your teeth may end up cleaner after paying more attention!). The idea is just to be aware of what you are doing while you are doing it.

Try continuing with this mindful tooth-brushing for the next week.

Washing the dishes

You can use other routine activities such as making coffee, taking a shower, chopping vegetables or house-cleaning as mindfulness practices. One of the traditional activities mentioned by mindfulness teachers over centuries is that of washing dishes. I remember hearing from childhood the old Zen proverb:

'What is the meaning of life?' asks the student.
'Have you eaten your meal?' asks the teacher.
'Yes I have,' replies the student.
'Then go and wash out your bowl,' says the teacher.
At that moment the student is said to have found enlightenment.

The Vietnamese teacher Thich Nhat Hanh is a great advocate of mindful dish-washing. He says 'while washing the dishes one should only be washing the dishes' – being completely aware of the washing while you are doing it, and not even thinking about the result. You can try it; enjoying the warmth and soapiness of the water, the satisfaction as you clean things, the reflection of light on the plates.

Bringing mindfulness to daily activities like this brings us out of our rumination into the here and now. It can also help us to shift our feeling of boredom and impatience with so much of what we do in our daily lives, and encourage us to experience more appreciation and enjoyment of the simple tasks which we often perform so mindlessly.

Mindful daily activity

Choose a routine activity in your daily life – something you do every day such as taking a shower, washing dishes, or making coffee. For the next week, see if you can do it mindfully.

Bring an awareness to the activity each time you do it. If you are washing dishes, be present with washing dishes. Just be aware of what you are doing while you are doing it.

Your choice of 'mindful activity':

_____

_____

So often we go through our week with a feeling of resentment about the 'boring' chores we have to do – rushing to get through them, checking off to-do lists, perhaps trying to do several things at once. Could you appreciate and even enjoy the simplicity of these daily activities?

7. Body

We might think that mindfulness is all about the *mind* – and yes, becoming familiar with our patterns of mind is part of the journey. But one of the bedrocks of mindfulness practice is the *body*: learning or re-learning how to be fully inside our own body, to be *embodied*. The body brings us into the present moment. As we come back to it, again and again, it anchors us in the here and now. When we are fully aware of the body, our mind and body are synchronized. We are connected, and we are whole.

Our modern Western culture is increasingly disembodied. Many of us sit at computers all day, staring at screens, existing only from the neck up. We *seem* to have a lot of interest in the body – everywhere there are images of sex, of fitness clubs, and of beautiful bodies selling products. But if you reflect on these images, a lot of our culture is about looking at the body from the outside, trying to shape the body into our ideas about how it should be.

When we go running or to the gym or to pilates class we may push through pain to exert our control over the body. When we eat, how often do we find that 'our eyes are bigger than our stomach' or that we are satisfying cravings that have little to do with what the body really wants or needs?

In mindfulness, we practise feeling the body from the inside and listening to the messages it sends us. All of our experience is registered in the body – the experiences we like, and those that we don't. Our body is constantly clenching, bracing, releasing, opening, softening and closing as we react to our experience in each moment. We resist feeling things that are difficult, and this repeated tightening and bracing can create chronic tension in parts of our body – sometimes in more obvious parts like the shoulders or jaw; sometimes deep in the belly, solar plexus or chest. Often we are unaware of how the body is registering the story of our life and our experience in each moment.

Body in stress

- Sit quietly and bring awareness into your body. Feel your feet on the floor and your weight on the chair.

- Think of a stressful situation you've been in – not the most stressful event ever, but something manageable. You might remember giving a presentation, sitting an exam, or perhaps a harrowing car journey.

- Take a few moments to imagine the scene. Now notice any sensations in your body. Is there anywhere where you are clenching, bracing or tightening? Perhaps you feel a shakiness, or shallowness of breath, perhaps butterflies in the stomach, or some other sensations? Take note of how your body feels in this scenario.

Emotions in the body

If we bring awareness to the body, we see there is a close interconnection between our thoughts and emotions and our body sensations. Not just stress, but sadness, anger, joy, desire – whatever we feel – is registered in the body.

Each of these states has its own kind of raw energy, but much of the time we don't allow ourselves to feel it. When we experience fear or anger we may have a sense of discomfort, and immediately we try to get rid of it by pushing it away, ignoring it or reacting in some way – shouting, freezing, running or hiding. By learning to let ourselves feel these body sensations, including the difficult ones, we have the possibility of responding to our experience in a fresh way, rather than falling into our habitual patterns.

Why pay attention to the body?

- To bring yourself into the present moment

- To connect with your direct experience through the senses, rather than thinking *about* your experience

- To let go of 'thinking' mode and come back to 'being' mode

- To become more aware of your emotions and how they manifest as physical sensations – as you gradually let yourself feel the difficult sensations and emotions, you will discover you *can* handle them and that you don't have to repress them or act them out

- To rediscover the body as a home – a place you can trust and come back to. You can re-inhabit the body and feel its natural qualities of groundedness and stability.

Feeling your fingers

This is an exercise to explore the difference between thinking about the body and experiencing it from the inside.

- **Picture your fingers.** Without looking at them, take a moment to visualize them. Imagine the shape of them – are they short and stubby, or long and slender? What do the fingernails look like? Do you have any thoughts about your fingers – perhaps you like them, or dislike them? Take a few moments to see what comes to mind when you think about your fingers.

- **Bring awareness into them.** Let go of *thinking about* your fingers, and see what it's like to bring awareness *into* them instead – to *feel* your fingers from inside.

- **Bring your attention to your left thumb.** Are there any sensations there? Can you feel the contact of the thumb on your thigh, or the book, or wherever it is resting? Is there tingling, or numbness; does it feel hot or cold? Are there any sensations in the tip of the thumb?

- **Now bring your awareness to the other fingers of your left hand.** Can you feel contact between them, or

55

the feeling of air in the gaps? Do they feel moist or dry, cramped or relaxed, heavy or light? Can you feel the finger tips, the finger nails, the joints?

- **Expand your awareness to take in the fingers and thumb of the right hand.** Have a sense of all ten fingers: there's no special way you need to feel, just notice any sensations that are here. Then expand your awareness to take in the whole of your hands, and any sensations in the palms, the backs of the hands, the wrists.

- **Thoughts.** If your mind wanders off during the exercise, that's not a problem. Notice any thoughts that are triggered, and gently bring your attention back again to the hands.

Now let this awareness fade and take a few moments to reflect on the exercise. Did you notice any difference between *thinking* about the fingers, and *feeling* them from the inside? Was it easy or difficult to be present with the direct experience of your sensations?

 Mindfulness helps us to move from *thinking about* the body to *feeling* it from the inside: being fully *embodied*.

The body scan

The body scan is a practice which involves bringing our awareness slowly and deliberately to different parts of the body. We're training ourselves to pay attention in a mindful way:

- On purpose – placing our focus where we choose to place it
- In the present moment – noticing whatever sensations are in the body, right now
- Non-judgementally – opening our awareness to sensations even if they are difficult, and letting them be just as they are.

The purpose is not to become relaxed, or to get into any particular state, but just to bring a friendly inquisitiveness to whatever is here in the body, in this moment.

Body-scan: feet and legs

Here is another exercise to bring awareness into the body. This time you'll also practise 'breathing into' specific parts of the body. Don't worry if this doesn't make sense at first, just play with the idea and see how it feels.

You can do this practice sitting, or lying down on your back – either with legs outstretched or feet flat on the floor and knees up. Take some time after each instruction to explore the physical sensations. It may help to close your eyes after each section, or you could familiarize yourself with the whole exercise and then put the book aside.

- **Settling in**

  Start by feeling the weight of your body – notice all the places where you are in contact with the floor (or the chair, if you are sitting). Notice the movement of the breath in your body. You could place your hands on your belly, and bring your awareness to the sensations in your abdomen, rising and falling with each breath.

- **Left toes**

  Now bring your awareness down the left side of your body into your left toes, tuning into any sensations here. What can you feel, if anything, in each of the five toes? Perhaps tingling, cramping, warmth or cold, contact with the sock, or contact with the other toes? Or no sensations, just a feeling of blankness? You don't have to shape your experience in any way, just notice whatever is here in this moment.

  Now imagine or feel you can breathe all the way down your body into your left toes, and then breathe back up from the toes, out through the nose or mouth. Don't strain, but try playing with this for a few breaths – breathing down into the toes, and back out from the toes. Have a sense of the breath and the awareness moving together.

- **Left foot**

  On an out-breath, let go of your focus on the toes, and move your attention to other parts of the left foot in turn: the top of the foot, the sole, the heel, the ankle. Notice any sensations of tightness, softness, heaviness, pain – whatever is here. When you're ready, broaden your awareness to take in the whole of the left foot. Now play with the sense of breathing into the whole of the foot, and out again from the foot.

- **Left leg**

  Let go of your attention to the foot, and move your awareness slowly through the rest of the leg. Notice any sensations in the lower leg: the bony shin and the fleshy calf. Bring attention to the knee: the kneecap, the muscles and tendons, the soft underside. Move awareness to the thigh, perhaps feeling the heaviness of the big thigh-bone, the feeling of contact with clothing. Finally broaden your focus to having a sense of the whole left leg, as if you were shining a beam of light on the leg from the toes to the top of the thigh. Explore what it's like to breathe into the leg, with a sense of filling the whole leg with breath and awareness.

- **Right leg**

  Now take your focus to the right toes, then the right foot, then up through the right leg, as you did with the left. Play with 'breathing into' each region before you move away, imagining the breath flowing into and out from that area.

- **Thoughts**

  As with all mindfulness practice, don't worry if your mind wanders off. Each time, just notice your attention has wandered and gently escort it back to the body.

- **Resting**

  At the end, spend a few moments resting, bringing awareness back to the sense of the whole body sitting or lying here, and the movement of the breath.

  What was your experience of this body scan practice? Take a few moments to write down anything you noticed during the practice:

  _____

  _____

  _____

  _____

THINK ABOUT IT

Your attention has different settings like a camera: you can have a narrow focus (e.g. your little toe) or a wide focus (e.g. the whole leg).

Mindfulness helps you train this ability to zoom in and out, and to choose what you want to focus on.

Being with difficulties

What was your experience of that last exercise? Don't worry if you found it difficult – there is no 'good' or 'bad' way to do this practice. Here are a few of the challenges which often come up when we practise mindfulness of the body:

- *My body feels uncomfortable/painful.* See if you can be gently curious about the discomfort. Can you bring your awareness to the area of any difficult sensations with a kind inquisitiveness? Explore if it's possible to stay with these sensations for a few moments rather than pushing them away or ignoring them. Try 'breathing in' to any areas of intensity, coming up as close as feels possible with your awareness, exploring the edges, and moving away when you need to. Decide for yourself if and when you need to move your body to alleviate the sensation, letting the movement become part of your practice. If there is strong pain, can you notice other parts of the body which aren't hurting? For more on working with difficult sensations, see Chapter 13.

- *My mind keeps wandering.* This is natural. The practice is just to keep bringing your attention back, again and again, with good humour.

- *I feel irritated – it's not relaxing.* Whatever emotions come up, can you be inquisitive about them? How does your irritation feel in the body? Is there a place where you can feel it? The aim is not particularly to be relaxed or calm – just to 'be with' your experience whatever it is. If you are irritated, frustrated or bored, that's just your experience right now. See if you can allow it to be as it is. (For more on working with restlessness, boredom and other challenges see Chapter 16)

Full body scan

The full body scan is usually done lying down, and takes between 25 and 45 minutes. We bring our awareness to each part of the body, most often starting with the left toes and moving all the way up to the crown of the head. The body scan is commonly done with a teacher's voice to guide you, either in a live class, or using recorded audio. You can download a guided body scan at **www.introducingbooks.com/mindfulness**.

It's not easy to do a full body scan while trying to read instructions from a book. But if you'd like to get a feel for it, you can repeat the 'feet and legs' exercise above, and this time continue through the whole body.

- Settle into your body, as in the previous exercise, lying down, or sitting in a chair. Feel your weight and the contact with the floor, and the rise and fall of the breath in your abdomen

- Now begin your scan of the body. In each place, spend a few moments noticing whatever body sensations are here, and exploring 'breathing in' to the different regions. The exact order is not so important but move as systematically as you can without skipping around too much
  - Left leg: toes, foot, calf and shin, knee, thigh, whole leg
  - Right side: same as the left
  - Hips, buttocks and pelvic area
  - Back: lower, middle and upper
  - Torso: belly, mid-torso, chest
  - Arms (both together): fingers, hands, lower arms, elbows, upper arms, shoulders
  - Head: neck, back of head, ears, jaw, parts of the face, whole face, top of head.

- At the end of the practice, you can imagine yourself breathing through your whole body, from the crown of your head to the toes and back again. Have a sense of the breath washing through your body, reaching every cell. Finish by resting still for a few minutes, with a sense of the whole body breathing, present and complete.

- When you bring awareness into your body, you are learning to 'be with' whatever is here, including sensations which are uncomfortable. You can train yourself to be gently inquisitive about your sensations and let them be as they are.

- This can help you in stressful situations to 'be with' difficult feelings, rather than reacting, lashing out or running away.

8. Attitude

Acceptance

One of the most important aspects of mindfulness is the attitude we bring to the practice – an attitude of acceptance or non-judgement. This may be easy to understand intellectually, but is possibly the most difficult thing to practise.

We are always talking to ourselves – we have a running commentary as constant and breathless as the commentator at a football match. But what tone of voice are we using? If you listen to that commentator in yourself, how often is he or she telling you that things aren't as they should be, that you're not as good as you should be, or that something or someone should be different?

In meditation practice, if we look and listen clearly to this internal voice, we may find that we are always giving ourselves a hard time. If our mind wanders, we chastise ourselves. If we are sleepy or irritated or angry, we blame ourselves. Or we turn this criticism outward, blaming the environment, the teacher or the practices for not living up to our idea of how things should be.

In meditation, each time we notice the mind has wandered, the instruction is just to notice and to escort it back to the focus of meditation – with gentleness. This part is crucial. Notice your tone of voice – when you find you've become distracted, do you slap yourself down, or can you develop a kindness to yourself, even a sense of humour?

'Oops, look, there I go again', as a fond grandparent might look with humour on a small child who keeps toddling off and needs to be herded back again and again.

In meditation we have a situation where we can practise speaking kindly to ourselves, and accepting our states of mind, whatever they are. If our mind is busy, it's busy. If we're tired, we're tired. If we're irritated, we're irritated. We can let ourselves feel how we feel.

If we can practise this within the quiet situation of the formal meditation practice, we can start to be more accepting of ourselves in the rest of life, shifting our old habits and softening our tendency to always judge ourselves. By making friends with ourselves, we can also be more friendly and accepting to others (see Chapter 17).

SPEAKING FROM EXPERIENCE

Sarah
Sarah is in her twenties and works in events and media. She joined a mindfulness course after a stressful year of work followed by an equally stressful period of being unemployed.

The thing that encouraged me about mindfulness was the non-judgemental side of it. The most helpful thing was the idea of it being okay to not feel okay. That had real resonance for me. I've had problems with depression and there was a resistance from people like my mother who'd say, 'Oh you just need to eat a good meal!', rather than accepting that this is a real thing that exists.

So it really helped – the idea of it being okay for you to feel the way you're feeling, and understanding that they're not unique thoughts anyway. The idea that it's okay to feel depressed or sad, rather than doing the British thing of sweeping it under the carpet or trying to fight it – they're both not particularly good strategies for dealing with the problem. If you can find a level of acceptance then you're on track to deal with it.

THINK ABOUT IT

Acceptance versus resignation

What reaction do you have to the word 'acceptance'? You may have a subconscious revulsion – perhaps it sounds too soft, too caring-and-sharing. You may feel that acceptance is equivalent to 'resignation' – giving up, being a doormat and letting the world trample you down.

This is not the kind of acceptance we're talking about. Acceptance is seeing clearly how things are, and not struggling with that basic reality. It doesn't mean that we can't take action against injustice or wrongdoing in the world. Once we have seen clearly and accepted what is here, then if there are things we can helpfully change, we can take action. In the words of the famous Serenity Prayer:

Grant me the serenity to accept the things I cannot change, the courage to change the things I can, and the wisdom to know the difference.

67

Mindfulness helps us to allow the space for this natural wisdom to emerge.

Animal taming

Mindfulness practice has often been likened to the taming of an animal. The human mind is wild and erratic: it takes skill and discipline to train it, but also patience and kindness.

There's a series of Buddhist pictures, used from the 12th century onward, which depict a young boy herding an ox or bull as a metaphor for this process of training the mind. At first the ox struggles and escapes frequently, and the boy has to put a lot of effort into bringing it under control. Later the ox becomes more gentle and obedient, and the boy is shown riding on its back while playing a flute.

Another metaphor is that of taming a wild horse – not by whipping it into shape, but by becoming familiar with the animal, discovering how to ride its energy, and guiding it back onto the trail when it tries to gallop off. If oxen and horses are rather far removed from your world, you may prefer the analogy of a puppy, bounding with energy, which can gently be trained to heel and to come when it's called. Whatever animal you imagine, it won't be tamed by shouting, but by using a voice that is kind and firm – and this is the tone of voice you can cultivate within your mindfulness practice.

TRY IT NOW!

Animal taming

Take a few moments to reflect on how your mind is feeling in this moment. (If you like, practise mindfulness of breathing for a few minutes first.) Is it leaping about from one thing to another, or wandering slowly, or staying still? Does it feel sharp and awake, or dull and heavy? You don't need to judge it as 'good' or 'bad', just notice.

If your mind in this moment were an animal, what animal would it be? A monkey? A wild horse? A sniffer dog? A pigeon? Or perhaps something slower – a snake, a lizard, a slug? Is this a familiar state of mind for you? Are there other animals which might represent your state of mind at other times?

How would you talk to this animal to encourage it – would you coo or cluck or whisper? Or perhaps there's a funny little voice you use when you talk to cats and dogs?

My mind is like:

_____

Next time you find yourself getting a bit too serious or heavy with yourself in your meditation, you could perhaps picture this animal and remember to develop humour and kindness in the way you speak to yourself.

Letting go

In nature, things take their own time to unfold – seeds grow, eggs hatch, butterflies emerge, all in their own good time. Likewise our mindfulness practice will take its time to unfold naturally, if we can be patient and open to each moment.

There is a paradox about meditation which is challenging to grasp. We have to put energy and work into the practice, and yet at the same time we have to let go of wanting results or trying to 'get somewhere'. For example, if you are trying to get more calm and relaxed, you are only setting up a struggle, and a feeling that things are not okay as they are. Within the discipline of our practice, we cultivate a kind of 'non-doing' – a willingness to be with things as they are. For control freaks this can be challenging! However, we can start to let go of our need to control everything and trust that our minds and the world are basically okay.

As we become more familiar with our mind, we discover that there are thoughts and feelings we want to cling to. They may be pleasant daydreams, or sometimes the nasty, juicy emotions have the strongest hold on us. In mindfulness, we practise letting go of these thoughts and experiences, whatever form they take, and coming back again and again to the focus of our meditation. As we practise, we may find that we are a little more able to let go of these attachments in the rest of our life. This letting go is a bit like the moment at night when we drop our mental chatter to fall asleep – only now we are practising it while we are awake.

The piece of advice I found really useful is that whatever's happening in the practice is what's happening. So if you're completely bored and frustrated and thinking, 'What the f--- is this about?', that's the meditation. That particular meditation is 'I think this is a load of shit, I don't know why I'm even trying.' If you're feeling calm or feeling angry that's how you're feeling. The practice is just being how you are at that moment. And that's hugely liberating – actually experiencing what's going on without an expectation for it to be different. If you do that a little tiny bit each day, I don't know how it works, but you will find that you feel very different after a while.

IF YOU REMEMBER ONE THING
The attitude you bring is a key part of mindfulness. Instead of wanting things always to be different, you let yourself be open to things as they are.

71

9. Feet

Do you have your head in the clouds? Or are your feet on the ground? We take these as metaphors, but they arise from a common experience which is quite literal and physical.

Take a moment to reflect on the contrast between these states. What does it feel like to 'be in your head', in the highest part of your physical body, with the sense of being caught up in the 'clouds' of your own thoughts? And then how does it feel to be grounded, to literally feel the connection of your feet to the ground, your weight going down into the earth?

In mindfulness, whatever practice you are doing, you begin by 'grounding' yourself, just as a building begins with the ground, the foundation. If you are doing a practice lying down, you can start by feeling which parts of the body are connected to the floor, and by being aware of the weight of your body. In a sitting position, the same thing applies – you can feel your feet on the earth (or your ankles, if you are sitting cross-legged), and the weight of your buttocks on the chair or cushion. If you are standing – doing a movement practice, or even waiting at the bus stop – you can begin by focusing your awareness into the feet.

This contact with the earth brings us into the present moment, and brings us down, down, down … out of the bulb at the top of our necks where many of us think we reside, until we can fully inhabit our bodies from the ground up. My own experience is that the simple act of bringing awareness into my feet is one of the most powerful mindfulness practices. It counteracts my tendency to get speedy and 'heady', and I do it many times throughout the day.

Mountain pose

- Stand in a simple upright position with your feet hip-width apart, your knees a little bent, your spine tall, the crown of your head lifted, and your shoulders relaxed. In yoga this is called the mountain posture.

- Feel every part of your feet in contact with the floor. Notice the connection of your ten toes, the padded balls of your feet, the outside edges, the arches, the heels. Feel the weight of your body going down through your feet into the earth.

- Try shifting your weight a little to the left and right, front and back. Then find a balanced place at the centre. Feel the sense of stability, and perhaps notice also that you are never completely still – you will likely sense little shifts and movements as you maintain your balance.

- Spend a few minutes tuning in to the sensations in your feet and the feeling of contact with the earth.

Mindfulness of walking

The act of walking is a skill which took us weeks or months to learn as a child, perhaps toddling uneasily from one piece of furniture to the next, and falling down. As a species it took us many millennia to get up and move on our hind legs. Yet now we take this process for granted, and do it without thinking. Mindfulness of walking is about bringing our awareness back into this remarkable activity which we do so much in our lives.

Walking meditation can be one of the most enjoyable forms of mindfulness practice, and has the advantage that you can do it without taking extra time out of your day. Any time you need to get from A to B, you can use the act of walking as a way to bring yourself out of your head and into the present moment. You can also do it as a practice in its own right, taking a few minutes out at any time for a mindful walk around the room or around the block.

At first it's good to try mindful walking in a private place where you don't feel self-conscious, and to start at a slow pace to get the feel of it.

Mindful walking

- Start by feeling the earth beneath your feet. As already discussed, you can feel all the different parts of your feet connecting to the ground, the weight of your body going down, the sense of gravity.

74

- Now transfer your weight into your left leg, noticing any sensations in your legs and feet as your right leg empties out and weight goes into your left foot. Slowly let your right heel come off the ground, and then the whole of your right foot, tuning in to all the physical sensations in your feet and legs.

- Then take a step forward – feel your right foot move through the air. Place the heel, then the rest of the foot onto the floor, maintaining awareness of the physical sensations as you transfer your weight into your right foot and your left foot empties of weight.

- Continue walking, staying aware of the sensations in the soles of your feet as they make contact with the floor, and of any sensations in the muscles of the legs. Begin very slowly, and then when you feel comfortable you can gradually pick up the pace. You don't have to look down at your feet – they know how to walk.

- When your mind wanders off, just notice this, and gently escort it back to the sensations in your feet and legs. You can use the contact of your feet on the floor as an anchor to bring you back into the present moment, just as we used the breath in sitting meditation.

TRY IT NOW!

Mindful walking: out and about

- Next time you have a journey to do on foot, bring your awareness to the fact that you are walking. Start by feeling the contact of your feet with the ground and the sensations in your legs as you walk. When you begin, you may find it helpful to have your gaze somewhat downward.

- As your mind becomes more focused on the walking, feel free to raise your gaze and take in the environment around you. Notice the trees, people, shops, sky – whatever is here – while still keeping part of your awareness in your feet. If you find yourself getting caught up in thoughts, it may help to bring your awareness back to a more narrow focus on the feeling of your feet on the ground. As the mind steadies, you can open your awareness again to the sights and sounds around you.

- You can also try different paces – how does the experience change as you walk more quickly? Can you be mindful even when you are hurrying?

Once you have a feel for it, mindful walking can be done at any speed, and you don't need to look like a zombie while you are doing it!

Experiment with walking mindfully for the next day or two. Walking is something most of us do often – commuting to work, going out to the shops, rushing from one meeting to another. Instead of letting yourself be wrapped up in the next thing you have to do, try using it as a chance to come out of automatic pilot and be present for a few minutes.

Mindful walking can provide a sense of space within a busy day, and can leave you feeling calmer and less exhausted when you arrive at your next destination. If you can really bring awareness to this simple act, it will provide a thread of mindfulness which will help you to become more present and awake in your everyday life.

- Bringing awareness into your feet helps you to be literally 'grounded' – to come out of your head and feel your connection to the ground.

- Like the breath, you can use your feet as an anchor, a place you can return your awareness to again and again. Through this simple act you become present inside your own body and awake to where you are right now.

10. Reacting

*We like reactions – a reaction is walking out on us, a
reaction is throwing tomatoes at the stage, that's a healthy
psychological reaction. I don't care how they react, as long
as they react.*

Alice Cooper

Whatever we encounter in life, there are three basic reactions we may have: like, dislike and indifference. These instinctive reactions may be so conditioned and habitual that we don't even notice them consciously, yet they dictate how we filter our experience throughout our lives. We have the fresh, direct experience of the world through our senses, and then immediately one of these three will kick in:

- **Attachment** – liking things, craving the things we like, wanting to hold onto the experiences we find pleasant

- **Aversion** – disliking things, pushing away the things we don't like, wanting to avoid the experiences we find unpleasant

- **Indifference** – switching off from the things and experiences that we don't notice or find of interest.

In mindfulness training we are not trying to stop or deny our reactions, but we can become more aware of them, and notice how they affect our mind and body, and our behaviour. We can open ourselves more and more to the direct experience of our world, beyond our habitual reactions. And as we practise, we may find ourselves more able to respond to things in a fresh way, instead of reacting automatically.

Seeing your reactions

Wherever you are – in your house, on a train, in a café – take a few moments to look around. You could scan the scene as if you were a film camera, panning slowly from left to right, and back again. Let your eyes take in whatever is here – objects, people, colours, shapes, textures, light and shade.

See if you can notice your reactions. Are there certain colours, objects or people you feel attracted to – things you naturally like? Are there other things you find unpleasant and would like to push away? Is there a third category of things you feel neutral about, perhaps don't even notice when you first look? You may find your reactions are strong, or they may be subtle – either way, just notice them.

Things you like

As Julie Andrews sings, we all have our favourite things which make us feel good. However, as we crash through life on automatic pilot, we may find that we're missing out on fully experiencing these moments which make up our life.

Moments you like

- Over the next few days, see if you can notice experiences that feel enjoyable while they are happening. They can be small and simple – drinking a cup of tea, seeing a big full moon, having a laugh with your colleague.

- Notice what thoughts and emotions are coming up. Also notice how you feel in your body. How can you tell that something is enjoyable, pleasurable, an experience you 'like'? Are there signals from your body – perhaps places where you feel a sense of relaxation, or lightness, or other sensations?

- Keep a note of each experience in as much detail as you can:

The experience	How I experienced it
E.g. I arrived home and saw the sun setting at the end of my road.	Thoughts: how beautiful – I'm glad I stopped to notice this. Emotions: happy, peaceful. Body sensations: shoulders relaxed, lightness in my chest, mouth smiling.

This exercise and the next one are inspired by Jon Kabat-Zinn's 'Awareness of Pleasant or Unpleasant Events Calendar' in his pioneering book *Full Catastrophe Living*.

When you begin to notice these little events in your daily life, here are some of the things you can learn about yourself:

- **Your reactions.** Becoming more aware of how the direct experience of your senses is immediately followed by a feeling of liking, disliking or ignoring.
- **Your thoughts, emotions and body sensations.** Noticing how your experience is made up of these different components, which are interlinked and constantly affecting each other. Sometimes you may be more aware of one or another, but usually all are present.

- **How pleasure registers in your body.** How do you know that an event is pleasurable? Can you start to notice the specific sensations which tell you: perhaps a feeling of your chest opening and lightening, your face relaxing, the corners of your mouth turning up, your shoulders dropping down?
- **Appreciating your world.** You may find that your life is full of sources of enjoyment which you haven't been noticing. By the simple act of tuning in to these experiences, your world can become richer and more nourishing.

(You might like to return to this section later on, when you've had time to do the exercise.)

Things you dislike

You may find it comes more naturally to notice the difficult experiences in your day. The traffic jam, or the meeting where your colleague is rude to you – these things can stick in the mind long after they're over. But can you notice a bit more about what's going on in those moments? What kind of signals does your body send you when you are experiencing something you don't want to experience?

Moments you dislike

It may be easiest to try this exercise after you've already spent some time with the experiences you like; or you can choose to notice both during the same period.

- During the course of a few days, see if you can notice experiences which are difficult, stressful or unpleasant while they are happening. It might be an argument with your partner, a nerve-racking moment at work, or a crowded ride on the train

- Notice what thoughts and emotions arise, and how the experience feels in your body. Do you notice any place where there is tension, shakiness or other sensations?

- Write down the details as soon as you can:

The experience	How I experienced it
E.g. Someone pushed in front of me in the queue at the supermarket.	Thoughts: I always get pushed around. I should be more assertive. Emotions: angry and helpless. Body sensations: jaw clenched, stomach tight, shoulders hunched and tight.

When you've done the exercise, here are some things you could begin to be more aware of:

- **Your reactions.** As with the more enjoyable events, noticing how your experience is constantly triggering reactions of liking, disliking and indifference.

- **Your thoughts, emotions and body sensations.** Each experience triggers all of these things. How do they interact?

- **How unpleasant experience registers in your body.** How do you know that you're experiencing something as unpleasant? What can you notice about the specific sensations which tell you this? Perhaps they include a feeling of clenching in the belly or solar plexus, a tightness in the chest or shoulders, a throbbing in the temples or tension in the jaw?

- **Being with difficult things.** You may notice that when you don't like something your body reacts by bracing, clenching, tightening, and generally trying to resist the experience or push it away. This resistance is actually making things worse and is part of what you experience as 'unpleasantness'. By bringing your awareness up close to these difficult sensations – being gently curious about them and giving them your attention – they begin to have less power over you. When your reactions are automatic and unconscious, they can rule the way you think and behave without you knowing it. When you bring these reactions into awareness, they are more able to pass through you and dissipate, without setting off a habitual chain of stress and negative thinking.

Things you ignore

The third type of reaction – indifference – gets less press than the other two but can be just as prevalent in our lives. A friend recently came running out of a cafeteria in tears because a group of people had ignored her. 'I sat down and they wouldn't speak to me – they were talking to everyone else!' Rather than deliberately slighting her, it's likely they just hadn't noticed her – maybe because she was not so interesting to them, or perhaps because they were wrapped up in their conversation.

With more mindfulness we may notice people or things which are right in front of our noses, which we have blanked out without realizing it. When we're indifferent to things it can be easy to switch off from the present moment and withdraw into our thoughts. As mindfulness brings us back to the here and now, we may discover a new richness in aspects of the world which had seemed uninteresting.

Reacting versus responding

Our reactions to experiences can be subtle or dramatic – and we all have our own style. When the really difficult stuff happens, some of us shout and throw things, and some of us run and hide.

What's your habitual reaction when things get stressful? What do you do when you have a big argument with your partner, or a disaster at work? Have a look at the list below. Do any of these resonate with you?

- Withdraw/hide/run away
- Shout/get angry
- Freeze
- Panic
- Clench my stomach/chest/shoulders/jaw
- Feel hurt/lost/lonely/abandoned
- Blame myself/blame others
- Drink alcohol/drink coffee/eat/smoke
- Overwork/get busy

Take a moment to reflect on which of these words and phrases feels most familiar to you, or choose some words of your own. How do you feel in your body when you're in the midst of this reaction?

As you may have noticed when you were paying attention to moments you dislike, when we experience something difficult, our body resists it by clenching, bracing, tightening and so on. We may feel other symptoms as the body's natural stress response kicks in: increased heart-rate and blood-pressure, sweaty palms, butterflies in the stomach. All of this feels uncomfortable and we try to get rid of these feeling by lashing out, running away, or whatever happens to be our pattern.

In mindfulness, we go against the natural reaction to turn away from these feelings, and instead we turn towards them. We allow ourselves to be with this uncomfortable energy – the adrenaline, the tension, the palpitations. Strangely, as we do this, there's a sense in which the energy of our anger, panic or grief can be allowed to exist and then move on through us, rather than being compounded by our resistance and attempts to get rid of it.

With mindfulness practice, we start to become more aware of our experience as it is happening. This creates a space in which we can have more choice about what we do next. Instead of 'reacting' automatically, we can start to 'respond' more mindfully – less destructively, and more skilfully.

- We are constantly reacting to our experience in three ways: liking, disliking and ignoring.

- We can tune in to our body sensations to become more aware of these reactions as they are taking place.

- Instead of avoiding difficult sensations, we can start to let ourselves feel them. This creates a space in which we can respond mindfully instead of reacting automatically.

---

11. Movement

We've begun the practice of bringing awareness into the body in relative stillness – sitting, lying or standing. We've also tried a moving meditation, mindfulness of walking. Now we can extend this to bring our mindfulness into other kinds of movement. As our bodies are naturally in motion for much of the day, movement practices can be a bridge between our formal meditation practice and the rest of our life.

Here are some reasons for practising mindful movement:

- **Being in the body in motion.** As you learn to bring more awareness into your body when it's moving, this can help you to be more present during the many kinds of movement you experience in daily life.

- **Exploring your 'edge'.** You can gently explore your body's natural limits by paying close attention to your physical sensations moment by moment as your body moves. You can play with finding your 'edge', that place where you are coming up to the edge of what's uncomfortable without pushing into it or beyond it. It's a practice of listening to the wisdom of your body, instead of overriding it with your mind. You may begin to see your habits and notice if you have a tendency to strive too hard, or to give up too easily.

- **Being with sensations.** As you explore the edge between comfort and discomfort, you can make your own choice in each moment about how close you want to get to difficult sensations, playing with going a bit further or coming back a bit. This is something you can also start to explore with other kinds of challenging feelings – including intense emotions.

 Mindful movement: standing stretches
The purpose of this practice is to bring awareness to the sensations in your body as it moves, and to gently explore the edge of what's comfortable or uncomfortable in each moment. Listen to your own body and don't do anything which is not right for you. If you have any physical problems do check with your doctor or physiotherapist before you do any kind of movement practice. You can perhaps do the movements in your mind, or choose different movements which are okay for you.

- **Mountain pose.** Begin by standing tall, with feet hip-width apart and knees slightly bent. As in the previous mountain pose exercise, feel the connection of your feet to the earth. Let the weight of your body sink into the ground, and the crown of your head lift towards the sky. Have a sense of the space your body is taking up and the space around you – be present.

- **Extending the arms.** Turning your palms away from your body, slowly raise both arms out away from your sides and up towards the sky, remembering to keep breathing. When the arms reach the top, try reaching higher through the fingertips, stretching both sides of the body. See if you can keep the shoulders down and relaxed. Notice any body sensations, and play with finding your 'edge' of comfort.

- When you're ready, slowly lower your arms back down again until they reach your sides, paying attention to the changing sensations on the way down, noticing the muscles being used in this movement. In mountain pose, notice any after-effects of the stretch.

- Repeat the same motion a few times, less slowly, breathing in as you extend your arms upward, breathing out as you lower them down.

- **Side stretches.** Again breathe in and raise your arms; this time keep them there. Tilt from your waist towards the right, reaching your arms up and over to the right, so you can feel a stretch through the left side of your body. If there's any intensity of sensation try 'breathing in' to those areas, seeing if you can soften and open up to the sensations. Gently explore your edge, where you are stretching yourself but not straining. Play with that edge, coming up to it, perhaps going a bit further and coming back again – listening to what your body (not your mind) is telling you to do.

- Breathing in, come back to centre and take the stretch to the left side, again exploring your edge. When you're ready, bring your arms back to centre and lower them down by your sides.

- **Shoulder rolls**. Gently lift both shoulders up toward your ears, then forward, then down, then back, making little circles, and remembering to breathe. Notice any places of tension or tightness – not forcing anything, just lubricating the shoulders very gently. After a few rolls reverse the direction, taking the shoulders up, back, down, then forward, keeping your awareness with the sensations.

- **Mountain pose.** Come back to stillness, and take a few moments to notice the effects of those movements on the body. Feel the connection of the feet to the earth again, the dignity of the upright posture and the sense of being present inside your own body.

Take a few moments to write down anything you noticed during the mindful movement practice:

_____

_____

_____

Visit **www.introducingbooks.com/mindfulness** to download audio for a longer practice of mindful movement.

Your reactions

What was your experience of that short movement practice? When we're moving the body there seems to be more happening than when sitting or lying down, so you may enjoy this and feel it's 'easier to focus'. Or you may find that it brings you up close to awareness of your body's limits in a way that feels uncomfortable. Or possibly, if you're used to athletic activity, you may find it frustrating to slow down and pay attention to the more subtle messages of your body sensations.

As with other mindfulness practices, see if you can notice these judgements and then let them go. See if you can open your awareness to the direct experience of the body, beyond what your mental commentary is saying about it.

Yoga

Mindful movement can be practised in many forms, but it helps if the pace is fairly slow so we have time to fully experience the sensations of the body. In mindfulness training we often use yoga postures as the basis for movement practice.

Yoga was developed in ancient India as a form of moving meditation, with the aim of bringing body and mind into synchronicity. In fact the physical postures, known as *asanas*, are only one branch of a comprehensive approach to life which includes ethics and meditation practice. Traditionally the physical sequences are used to calm and focus the energies of the body and mind, preparing the practitioner for the stillness of meditation. Recently, of course, yoga has become popular in the West as a form of exercise, without necessarily being connected to any meditative purpose.

The great early writer on yoga was Patanjali, whose *Yoga Sutras* have been dated to around the 2nd century CE. Patanjali doesn't give detail about what postures to use, but he says that the practice should balance *sthira* (translated as steadiness, firmness or effort) with *sukha* (gentleness, comfort, or ease). In other words, there's a balance we can look for in each moment, between trying too hard and flopping out, and between strength and softness.

By working with relatively slow, careful movements such as yoga sequences, we can take the time to explore this edge within our own body. Instead of competing with ourselves, or trying to match some external image, we can pay attention to the information being given to us by our own physical sensations, finding the right place for our body in each moment.

As well as yoga, there are other traditions of slow, meditative exercise which are excellent to use for mindfulness of movement. These include the Chinese practices of Qigong and Tai Chi, both of which use slow moving sequences to direct the flow of energy in the body. These days almost every town offers classes in yoga or tai chi, and you can also find sequences in audio or video formats. For the purposes of developing your mindfulness of movement, choose a practice which is simple enough that you can focus on your body sensations, rather than trying to follow something which is overly complicated or athletic.

SPEAKING FROM EXPERIENCE

Tessa

I took up yoga when I was working too much on the computer and I started to get RSI in my arm – my brother had RSI and told me yoga was the most helpful thing. After a day sitting rigid working on websites, it was a wonderful feeling to get everything moving and flowing again.

I've always enjoyed outdoor sports but somehow the slower, meditative quality of yoga started to bring me into my body in a way I'd never felt before. I was already a meditator at this point, but over time I noticed a change. I used to talk about *watching* my breath, and it seemed to be something happening mainly up in my head. Now I started to really *feel* the breath moving deep down in other parts of my body like my belly. And when I did walking meditation, I often used to be impatient and want to go faster – now I could enjoy the feeling of all the parts of my foot making contact with the floor with each step, almost like a massage.

This feeling of being more in my body also affected my other physical activities. When I swim lengths, I can enjoy the movement of each stroke through the water, rather than getting bored or being off somewhere else in my thoughts. I'm better at tennis – I've discovered my body usually knows where it needs to be on the court, if I can get my mind out of the way. And the best of all, for me, is dancing – when you can stop worrying about other people or how you look, and let the body move the way it wants to move. It's one of the best kinds of moving meditation I know.

Mindful movement: your choice

Practise bringing mindfulness into your favourite form of exercise – it could be swimming, going to the gym, running, or dancing around your flat. See if you can bring awareness into your body sensations in each moment, and pay attention to the edges of your physical limits. If you find yourself caught up in thoughts, just notice that and return your awareness to the body.

Mindful movement: out and about

It's good to practise mindful movement slowly at first, and to set aside time for some kind of formal practice, so that we can focus on our body sensations without too much distraction. But then we can begin to bring this awareness into our body as we move through our daily lives – whether we're hoovering or gardening, carrying boxes or pushing a pram. We can also bring the qualities of mindful movement into other sports and physical activities such as running, tennis, cycling, football or dancing.

Awareness of physical movement, in whatever form, can be a powerful way to bring yourself into the present moment.

12. Sound

I have often lamented that we cannot close our ears with as much ease as we can our eyes.

Richard Steele

We live in a noisy world, surrounded by traffic, aeroplanes, music and people, hums and bleeps. You may think of meditation as a welcome escape into blissful silence. And certainly, it can be helpful to find a reasonably quiet place for your practice, where you are not too distracted by constant sounds.

At the same time, it's perfectly possible to meditate with noise around us. When we hear a neighbour shouting or a dog barking, we can let this be part of our awareness. We can even go further and practise mindfulness of sounds, where the field of hearing becomes the main focus of our attention.

Mindfulness of sounds
- Sitting with upright posture, take a moment to feel grounded. You may like to close your eyes.

- Now turn your attention to sounds. There's no need to go out and hunt for sounds, just allow them to come to you. There may be sounds up close, in your body, in the room, outside or far away.

- Notice the pitch, the texture, the loudness – and the gaps between sounds, silence. See what it's like to be with the direct experience of sound, rather than *thinking about* the sound, as if you were a microphone, just receiving the sounds from wherever they come.

- If your mind wanders, bring it gently back to awareness of sounds. If you find yourself creating a storyline around the sound, see if you can come back to the simple experience of hearing.

- Notice how the sounds come, sometimes stay around for a while, and then go. Sounds arising and dissolving within the wider space of your awareness.

You may notice that sounds trigger all kinds of thoughts, perhaps trying to figure out what they are ('Is that hum the heating or the fridge?'); weaving storylines ('They must be having another party next door …') or naming and labelling the sounds ('Clock, washing machine, birds, children …'). There's nothing wrong with any of this, but when you notice you're caught up in thoughts *about* the sounds, see what it's like to come back to the direct experience of sound itself.

Direct experience versus concepts

In what is seen, there is only the seen
In what is heard, there is only the heard
In what is sensed, there is only the sensed
In what is thought, there is only the thought

Bahiya Sutta

Through mindfulness of sounds – and indeed any other mindfulness practice – we can notice this difference between *direct experience* and *thinking about* our experience. It's not that the thoughts and concepts are bad; they are useful and necessary for us to function and to be creative. But the direct experience of our senses is always happening here and now, and brings us into the present moment. Reconnecting with direct experience brings us a fresh appreciation of the little things which make up our everyday life. Over a lifetime, our concepts and thought patterns can become narrow, predictable and limited. Direct experience opens us up to a wider and more vivid world.

Reacting to sounds

Mindfulness of sounds can also be a good training ground for becoming more aware of our reactions to our experience, as discussed in Chapter 10. You might notice that you have constant reactions to sounds – some you like, some you dislike, and some you don't mind one way or the other.

You may have a strong physical reaction to some sounds. When you hear a loud, unexpected noise, do you find yourself clenching your stomach, or perhaps bracing your body against the sound in some way? These reactions – to sounds and other stimuli – are happening constantly below the radar of our consciousness. The regular act of bracing, clenching, tightening and so on creates tension in our bodies which we carry around without realizing it. When we bring more awareness to our reactions, as we saw in Chapter 10, we may find that they have less hold over us. We are opening up space to other possibilities in the way we relate to our experience.

When we come back to the direct experience of sound, we can try dropping our judgement about it and being curious – what is the texture and pitch? Do the sounds stay the same or change? Are there layers of sound or is it one tone? Try listening this way even to sounds you think you hate, such as traffic. You may find that the sound of traffic, stripped of our judgement about it, has something in common with a sound that we 'like' such as a waterfall or waves on the shore. (Or you may not! There is no right or wrong way to hear things.)

When we have worked in this way directly with sounds, we can use this approach when they come unbidden into other mindfulness practices. For example, we may be practising mindfulness of breath when our flatmate starts making loud clattering in the other room. Instead of letting it trigger us into irritation or anger, we can hear the sounds as just that – sounds. If we do have a reaction, we can notice that – for example, are there any sensations in the body? Then we bring our awareness back to the breath, or whatever is our main focus. We can let the sounds be part of the background, allowing them to be there in our awareness, without needing to fight with them or push them away. This is an excellent practice in cultivating acceptance of how things are, and welcoming our experience as it is, rather than constantly resenting the world for not being the way we want it to be.

Mindfulness of sounds and reactions

- Repeat the exercise above. This time, also pay special attention to any reactions you may have – 'liking' some sounds and 'disliking' others.

- If there are sounds you find unpleasant, notice any reactions you may have in your body – perhaps some tightening or bracing against the sound. You might like to try softening and breathing into the area where there is bracing, and notice if that has any effect on being with the sound. See if you can be especially inquisitive about these less pleasing sounds. Examine the pitch, tone and texture; and notice whether they are constant or changing. Be curious and explore what it might be like to allow the sounds to be as they are.

Sounds and space

Another thing to notice about sounds is the way that they come and go within the wider space of our awareness. Some sounds are close, some right inside our bodies, while some are very far away. We may begin to sense an enormous space, and we may sense that we can rest our awareness in this space. The sounds come and go, but our minds are not the sounds, they are the space in which the sounds arise and dissolve. Our awareness is vast and stretches out in all directions.

This sense of the spaciousness of awareness is one of the crucial discoveries of mindfulness – and although we can point to it with words, it is something that can really only be discovered through experience. Mindfulness of sounds can be a helpful practice to start getting a feeling of this natural spaciousness of our minds. We'll talk about this more in Chapter 14.

Mindfulness of sounds is a simple practice which can be done anywhere. You can use this practice to bring your awareness into the present moment, and to help you to notice:

- The difference between direct experience and concepts *about* that experience

- Your constant reactions to your experience – liking, disliking and ignoring

- The spaciousness of your awareness in which events like sounds come and go.

---

13. Sensations

Now, if you like, stop reading for a few seconds. Come out of your head and right down into your body. Feel your feet on the floor, and your weight on the seat. You can do this at any moment, coming back to being in your body.

Western education trains us to put a lot of emphasis on thinking – in Descartes' famous phrase, 'I think therefore I am.' Analysis, logical thinking and scientific reasoning are backbones of our belief system. Our pop songs express a different side of the story – 'What a feeling!', 'Feeling groovy', 'Feelin' it', 'You've lost that loving feeling', 'I feel good'. But what does it mean to feel?

The word 'feeling' can mean both a physical sensation, and an emotional state. In mindfulness training it can be helpful to make a distinction between 'emotions' and 'body sensations'. Sometimes when you're in the midst of a 'feeling' it can be hard to distinguish between what is physical and what is emotional – they are so closely linked. Your anger, fear or desire can be like a weather system moving in – a particular kind of energy which takes you over. But if you can really tune in to how this energy manifests in the body, and be curious about it, it will help you to simply be present with the sensations and not react blindly in your habitual way.

Our culture emphasizes the value of words and concepts, and we're not always so good at experiencing our sensations. How can we become more sensitive to physical sensations, to the messages of our own body? It may help to explore which words might come closest to expressing your physical sensations.

Words and sensations

- Here are some words about sensations. Read slowly through the list. Are there any which resonate for you? Is there a part of your body which feels like this right now?

- Hot, cold
- Tight, loose
- Moist, damp, dry
- Soft, firm, hard, brittle, stiff
- Tense, tight, clenching, bracing
- Tingling, vibrating, shaking, pulsing
- Light, heavy, solid
- Contact, pressure
- Blank, numb
- Tender, sore
- Aching, cramping, painful
- Dull, sharp
- Full, empty
- Open, closed

- Pick a word which resonates for you right now. Your knee is aching? Your neck feels tight? Spend a few moments feeling these sensations. Do they stay the same when you bring your attention to them?

- If you like, repeat this exercise using another word. Feel free to use your own word which is not on this list.

- Pick one of the words which feels familiar to you, and see if you can notice those sensations when they come up during the rest of your day.

Your word or words:

_____

_____

Difficult sensations

Bringing this level of awareness into the body is not always a comfortable experience. It can be quite shocking to notice how much tension we're holding; how many aches and pains we've been trying to block out. But allowing ourselves to fully experience sensations in the body is a powerful part of our mindfulness practice. Our natural instinct is to push difficult sensations away, to fight with them or avoid them altogether. But in mindfulness we do the opposite, coming up as close to the sensation as feels possible in the moment (as we did in mindful movement) and becoming gently curious about the sensations.

We can train ourselves in opening to whatever is here, even if it is painful. The pain or tension may not go away, but we are no longer losing a lot of energy on fighting with it. Paradoxically, by giving it attention, the chances are the pain may begin to have less hold on us. We may find that it is less solid and less unbearable than we think it is.

It's good to experiment with this approach, but do so kindly. You could try practising first with mildly uncomfortable sensations, aches, itches and so on. If you feel overwhelmed, let go of exploring the difficult sensations and bring your awareness back to the weight of your body, or the movement of your breath. You can come back to the breath as a safe haven, and let yourself be stabilized by its natural movement at any time when other sensations or emotions are feeling too much to handle. Then, from that steady, grounded place, see if you can open to exploring the sensations again.

Mindfulness of difficult sensations

- Settle into a sitting posture which feels dignified and awake. Practise mindfulness of breathing for a few minutes.

- Now expand your awareness around the breathing to a sense of your body as a whole – from your feet on the floor to the crown of your head. Tune in to the feeling of the breath moving through your whole body, reaching every cell.

• Now notice if there are any difficult or uncomfortable sensations in any parts of your body, which are calling for your attention. Maybe tension in your neck, aching in your back, tiredness in your legs – or perhaps you have a more intense kind of pain. Instead of avoiding these sensations, see if you can gently bring your awareness up close to this region of intensity. Try coming up to the edges of it, moving away whenever you need to and coming gently back again when you're ready.

• Imagine you can breathe right into this area, carrying your awareness there. You are not trying to get rid of the intensity but to explore what's there by breathing into – and with – the sensations.

• Be curious about the sensations. Do they have a texture, a shape or even a colour? Are they sharp or dull, soft or hard, constant or changing? Are they like metal, or stone, or wood, or textile? Spend a few minutes gently exploring these sensations with your awareness, as much as feels possible.

• When you're ready, widen your awareness to having a sense of the body as a whole, from the feet to the crown of the head. If you've been working with some kind of pain, you could notice now the parts which aren't hurting. Feel the grounded, stable quality of the body. Return your awareness for a few minutes to the breath, and the sense of your body breathing.

Write down anything about your experience during this practice here:

_____

_____

_____

_____

You can incorporate this exercise into any of your mindfulness practices. When you find that strong physical sensations are distracting you, see what happens if you bring a kindly awareness to that region. Let yourself be inquisitive and open to the sensations, rather than pushing them away. Notice if there are other parts of the body where there is any resistance against the discomfort – perhaps a tightening of the shoulders, stomach or jaw? See if you can breathe into and soften around the resistance. Is this resistance or bracing adding an extra layer of pain on top of the original pain? What is left of the discomfort when the resistance is lessened?

Marion

Marion took up mindfulness practice looking for relief from the physical pain caused by her auto-immune condition (see Chapter 3). She remembers vividly the first time she tried bringing her awareness up close to the difficult sensations.

It was absolutely counter-intuitive. It was almost like stepping right up to another person and being an inch away from their nose – going right up to the pain and just being with it, just looking at it, just listening to it, just feeling it; without thinking 'I'm trying to reduce this or manage this.' Just saying, 'This is what's going on in my body at the moment.' What I found extraordinary was that after the meditation my relationship to the pain had changed.

Each time I do a meditation with pain it's completely different. Sometimes I feel like I'm almost wrestling with it, sometimes I'm almost dancing with it, sometimes I'm just chatting with it. Something does change when you go right up to it in a non-judgemental way – not with fear, not with a story. Not even with a story about being brave, not 'I'm going to face my pain!' – just seeing what's there.

Torso

Do you ever get butterflies in your stomach? Does your heart sometimes ache? Do you ever have a gut feeling?

When we have strong experiences like fear, grief and stress, they tend to register somewhere inside the torso.

Deep in the soft central parts of the body, all kinds of sensations are taking place, but often we don't pay attention to them. You may react to difficult experiences in your belly, or solar plexus, or chest. There may be one area which is particularly sensitive for you, or it may vary. If you can pay attention to these sensations, your body can give you early warning signals about how you are feeling in this moment, before your mind becomes fully conscious of it.

Our bodies have strong instincts for self-protection. We armour ourselves against feeling things we don't want to feel, and then this armour gets tighter and tighter – we can't digest properly, we can't breathe fully. The armour can become a kind of iron corset which stops us from relaxing and opening up to the world. Is this true for you? Can you feel a physical difference between being 'open' and being 'closed'?

Sensations in the torso

- **Mindfulness of breath.** Take up a good sitting posture and practise mindfulness of breathing for a few minutes.

- **Breath in the belly.** Bring your awareness especially into the movement of your breath in the walls of your abdomen, expanding on the inhale, and relaxing back again on the exhale. It may help to put a hand on your belly to feel the subtle rise and fall.

- **Belly.** Tune in to any other sensations in the belly area. Are there sensations of digestion? Feelings of emptiness or fullness? Is there any tightness? Or softness, openness?

- **Solar plexus.** Move your awareness up to the area just under the rib cage; your solar plexus and diaphragm. Can you feel your breath moving here? Notice any sensations: is there bracing, resisting? Or openness, relaxation?

- **Chest.** Bring your focus upward to your chest, and your breath moving here. Inside, do you have any sense of the organs working here: your lungs filling with air, the beating of your heart? What sensations can you notice in this area? Perhaps tenderness, shakiness, softness, openness? Or tightness, holding, numbness? There's no particular way you should feel, just see if you can be gently curious and allow things to be as they are.

- **Early warning signals.** Imagine for a moment a stressful or difficult situation. As you bring this to mind, is there somewhere you can feel a change of sensations in your torso? Perhaps a place where you clench or brace to protect yourself? Is this a familiar feeling? If so, take a note of this as a location where you may get early warning signals in your body. See if you can tune in to this place at other times in your day and notice what is going on here.

- **Mindfulness of breath.** To end the practice, return your awareness to the feeling of your breath moving in your body, and the sense of the whole body, sitting here breathing.

Write down anything which you noticed during this exercise. Is there a particular area which gives you signals that you are feeling stress or difficult emotions?

_____

_____

_____

_____

_____

_____

REMEMBER THIS!!!

- You can practise gently opening yourself to intense sensations and being curious about them. By coming towards them instead of pushing them away, they can start to have less hold on you.

- When difficult things happen, you may be reacting to this somewhere in your torso. See if you can tune in to these sensations as an early warning system.

- Notice if there's a different physical feeling of being 'open' to your experience, compared with the feeling of being 'closed'

14. Thoughts

In practising mindfulness we don't see thoughts as a problem. We can start to make friends with them and see their patterns. We're not trying to get rid of them to achieve an empty mind. They are as natural as waves, coming and going within the ocean of our awareness. But in the normal course of life, we tend to be swept away by our thoughts, experiencing them as more solid and real than they actually are. We buy into them, we believe them, we let them fill up our reality and tell us what to do. We think our thoughts and our selves are the same thing. Through meditation practice, we can start to see that thoughts are not so solid, and that they are not 'us'. We can begin to let go of them, and to loosen their hold on us.

We can practise cultivating a new relationship to our thoughts within any of our mindfulness practices. Each time our mind wanders off, sooner or later we notice that, and gently bring it back to the focus of attention – whether it's the breath, body, sounds or some other focus. We cultivate a kind tone of voice in the way that we do this, so that we don't see thoughts as the enemy. But we can also see through them, and realize that they are insubstantial and impermanent.

Isaac

Isaac is a teacher and consultant in his 40s, who meditates regularly.

It's always really interesting seeing my patterns of thought. It's like a soap opera. You re-live last week's episode: 'Previously, on Isaac … and now, on Isaac.' Often there's worry about family, or whether I did a good enough job at work. Sometimes being in love can be quite epic. And there's always emotional baggage connected with other people. Maybe somebody said something in a particular way – 'Did they really mean it like that? They just walked off … what did I say wrong?'

Or for me 'messing up' is quite a big one. I have this tendency to torture myself with any mistake that I've had the audacity to make, replaying it over and over again, in different permutations. In the end you have to laugh.

Labelling thoughts

Some meditation traditions encourage a practice of 'labelling' thoughts. This helps us to be clearer about the difference between when we're caught up in a thought and when we are present with the focus of our meditation. At the very moment when you notice you've been caught, you can say silently to yourself 'thinking', before you return to the breath or other focus. This can be especially helpful when you've been off in a daydream, away with the fairies for some time, and suddenly – here you are again in the room. By acknowledging 'thinking' at this point, you are bringing in an element of precision, and marking the moment of returning to your focus.

In this process, remember not to judge the thoughts as good or bad. Whether you've been thinking about how you'd like to murder your partner, or dwelling in deeply spiritual reflections on the meaning of life, it's all just 'thinking'. You also don't get into analysing your thoughts, although you may notice their flavour a little bit. You may see how some thoughts keep coming back, or how you're tending towards a particular kind of thought such as planning, worrying, or daydreaming. But above all, as you label 'thinking' you are acknowledging your willingness to let go of the thought, however juicy or compelling it may be. There may be another time and place for thinking about this subject, but during the meditation practice, you are willing to come back to simply being present with your body or your breath, here in this moment.

Mindfulness of breathing: labelling thoughts

- Sit in a comfortable, upright position which embodies dignity and wakefulness. Feel the contact of your feet on the floor and the weight of your body.

- Bring your awareness to your breath. Spend 5 to 10 minutes practising mindfulness of breathing.

- From time to time, and perhaps often, you will notice that your attention has been taken away from your breath. Each time you notice this, say silently to yourself 'thinking', and then return your awareness to your breath. See if you can do this without judgement, cultivating a kindly tone of voice, and even a sense of humour. 'Ah, thinking again!'

- Do this each time your mind wanders, as often as you need. Don't judge the thoughts as good or bad. Each time just label them 'thinking' and return to the breath.

Thoughts as clouds

As we continue our practice, we may become more curious about thoughts: what they are and how they behave. We may find that our awareness is like a big space into which thoughts come and go. Our mind is like a vast blue sky, and the thoughts are like clouds, some of them small and wispy, some of them thick, black and heavy. The clouds may seem to fill the sky, but we begin to understand that we are not the clouds; we are the sky which holds them.

Modern psychology makes a distinction between these different aspects of our mind. We have the process of thought, or cognition, and overseeing this we have meta-cognition. Meta-cognition is the process of knowing about knowing – an awareness that can shine a light on the whole of our experience, including our thinking processes.

This affirms a distinction made by Buddhism, which for centuries has taken a great interest in the workings and processes of the mind. Tibetan Buddhism distinguishes between *sem*, or small mind and *rikpa* or big mind, the mind of wisdom. Small mind is the constant chattering as we talk to ourselves, and big mind is the wider field of awareness within which this commentary takes place.

We experience big mind, or *rikpa*, when there are gaps in our chatter. Pema Chödrön likens this to the constant yelping of dogs she experienced during the night-time in Nepal (small mind) ... and the deep silence when all the dogs stopped barking for a moment and there was stillness (big mind). As she says, we are not trying to get rid of the dogs, but in meditation we may sometimes find that our mind settles down so that there is just an occasional yip and yap instead of a constant canine cacophony. (At other times the cacophony continues, and we can start to accept the beauty of that too!)

Mindfulness of thoughts

We've practised how to work with thoughts when they appear within our mindfulness practice, taking us away from the object of focus. We can also bring thoughts onto centre stage as the main object of our meditation. This can be a good practice to try after working with mindfulness of sounds, as there is a similar quality to the experience. Just as we notice sounds coming and going within the space of our awareness, we can see how thoughts also come and go within this bigger space of our awareness, arising and dissolving into this space.

Don't worry if this exercise is difficult for you – it's generally considered to be quite a challenging and 'advanced' form of meditation. Just have a go, in the spirit of an experiment. As always, it is good to start the practice by grounding ourselves and being present in the body.

 Mindfulness of breath, sounds and thoughts

- **Breath.** Take a comfortable, wakeful posture and feel your connection to the earth. For the first few minutes, bring your awareness to the movement of your breath in your body.

- **Sounds.** Now when you're ready, move your attention to sounds. Notice pitch, tone, texture, loudness – and gaps between sounds, silence. Notice how the sounds arise and dissolve within the wide space of your awareness.

- **Thoughts.** When you're ready, let sounds fade into the background, and move your awareness to thinking itself. Instead of seeing thinking as a distraction, allow yourself to notice each thought as it arises, perhaps stays around a while, and as it dissolves. It's as if you are the vast blue sky, spacious and clear, and the thoughts are clouds arising in that sky. Some are light and fluffy, some are heavy storm clouds. As best you can stay present, not trying to do anything with the thoughts. Just be aware of them, and let them come and go.

You may notice that some thoughts come laden with emotions, heavily charged. If so, can you notice any sensations in the body connected to the emotion? Perhaps you can feel a resistance to feeling this emotion, or thinking this thought – some kind of clenching or tightening in part of the body? As best you can, bring a gentle awareness and curiosity to whatever sensations are here.

• **Breath.** To end the practice, bring awareness back to your breath, and the sense of your whole body sitting here, breathing.

When you finish, you might like to write down anything you noticed during this practice:

_____

_____

_____

_____

What was your experience of this meditation? You might find yourself completely caught in the thoughts, without much sense of any space or 'blue sky' around them. Or you might have the opposite experience – suddenly when you are asked to pay attention to thoughts, none appear; your mind is blank. If that's the case, isn't that interesting? Can you rest in this experience of space, without thoughts, however momentary?

There is no right or wrong thing for you to experience. But by experimenting with turning our awareness directly to thoughts, we can encourage ourselves to be curious about their nature. We can start to get a glimpse of how our mind works, and see that the constant stream of images and conversations it throws up are no more substantial than the changing scenes of a movie on a screen. We may find ourselves swept up into the scene with the actors, but each time we can notice that and come back to our seat right here in the cinema. The more we do this, the more we may find that through all the dramas and storylines we are able to hold our seat.

Thoughts are not facts

The practice of looking clearly at our thoughts is an important part of Mindfulness-Based Cognitive Therapy, which was developed especially to help people with a history of depression. When we get into a state of depression, we have a tendency towards 'rumination': thought processes which go around and around, and can be very unhelpful.

There may be a chain reaction of thoughts, which starts with something small and leads us inexorably forward into deeply negative thoughts about ourselves and our lives.

For example, we make a mistake at work and we think:

'I don't know what I'm doing.'
'I can't get this done on time, I can't do this project.'
'Everyone knows I'm useless.'
'I'm going to get found out and lose my job.'
'I'll be out on the streets, I won't be able to get another job, I'll be penniless, I'll lose my home and security, I'll die poor and lonely …'

Most of us have our own version of this snowballing thought process, which leads each time to our own deepest worries or fears. It's a well-worn groove we can easily slot into, and once we're on that track, we travel on automatic pilot from the slightest trigger to the grim conclusion. Often these thoughts are subconscious, or only semi-conscious. A small event or remark can set off a reaction, and we find ourselves moments later feeling heavy and bleak, without being fully aware of what's happening. By bringing more awareness to the situation, we have the opportunity to interrupt our habitual reaction and create a chance for something fresh and different in our response.

TRY IT NOW!

Chain of thoughts

- Take a good posture, feel grounded, and spend a few moments in mindful breathing.

- Imagine a difficult scenario in your life at the moment – perhaps a conflict in your workplace, or a challenging relationship, or a worry about money. Choose something which is manageable, not too overwhelming. Bring your awareness to any emotions and body sensations which arise as you picture this situation.

- Now bring your attention to your thoughts. Is there a 'snowball' of thoughts that you experience in this situation? Write down the sequence of thoughts that come to you. Are there any familiar worries or fears coming up? See if you can notice any 'chain reaction' of one thought triggering another, as in the example above.

- Most of us find that there are certain underlying fears which are particularly familiar to us; dark thoughts we find ourselves arriving at, no matter what the specific scenario. Your particular version might be 'I'm useless', or 'Nobody loves me', or 'Everyone is against me', or 'I can't do anything right'. Take a moment to think about whether there are particular thoughts like this which feel familiar to you.

My chain of thoughts:

_____

_____

_____

_____

_____

Seeing thoughts as thoughts

Mindfulness-Based Cognitive Therapy offers some suggestions about how we might work with these unhelpful and destructive thoughts when we become aware of them. We can bring them into the bright light of day and challenge them, asking ourselves questions about the thoughts, such as:

- Am I making assumptions?
- Am I blaming myself for something which isn't my problem?
- Am I expecting something unrealistic from myself?
- Am I turning something small into a catastrophe?
- Is there another way of looking at this? How would a good friend advise me to look at it?

These can be helpful strategies, and the act of challenging negative thoughts is an important method used in Cognitive Behavioural Therapy (CBT). You may like to research and develop this approach further, particularly if you have a tendency to depression. And in general, if you find that a lot of thoughts and emotions are coming up which are hard to handle on your own, it could be good to find a friend who can help you talk it through – or perhaps look into some further support from a counsellor or therapist.

Whether we are depressed or just feeling a bit low, it can be very useful to bring our negative thoughts into the light of day, and to challenge them with practical questions like the ones above. However, the core teaching of mindfulness in relation to thoughts is very simple: see thoughts as thoughts; as mental events, no more or less. We begin to understand that the thoughts are not facts, and the thoughts are not us.

Through our training in formal mindfulness practice, we show ourselves willing again and again to see our thoughts as thoughts, and let go of them. We discover that we have a much vaster awareness – the 'big mind' which we can come back to and rest in at any time when the chattering and yelping of 'small mind' is overwhelming us. This can slowly begin to have a powerful effect on the way we relate to our minds and thoughts in daily life.

Anthony

Anthony was in his 50s working in a stressful job as a hospital chaplain and going through a marriage breakdown when he joined a mindfulness course.

My wife was saying that she wanted us to separate, and it was very shocking and upsetting. My experience is that when things are stressful I find it very easy to get taken out of myself into worry about what's going to happen. A lot of the time the thoughts are quite condemnatory and judgemental. The circling thoughts take me out of myself – in a sense I lose myself. Mindfulness brings me back to my centre, to me.

The practice helped me to come to new thoughts about what I should do in the situation. The usual thoughts go round and round in my head, but these other solutions seem to come almost physically from deep inside me. The mindfulness practice allows things to shift in a way that normal thinking never does.

Debbie

Debbie, now in her 40s, has been practising mindfulness for almost twenty years.

I used to get depressed, but since I started mindfulness I don't go into depression in the same way. I used to ruminate – I'd have negative feelings on top of negative feelings. If, for example, I thought 'I'm lonely', I'd then add

'I'm lonely and I haven't got a boyfriend, I'm never going to get a boyfriend, I'll always be on my own ...' and so on. I'd go into rumination and there's the snowballing effect.

Since then I've started to catch that quite quickly. So if I'm doing my practice I'm able to go 'Aha, it's this thing again!' So I cut through it before I go off into depression. I remember the first time I started actually catching myself having thoughts at the time I was having them – that was a bit of a eureka moment. I'd be feeling really overwhelmed but then have a watcher, another part of me able to see these things and have some space.

IF YOU REMEMBER ONE THING Through mindfulness practice we can learn to let go of our thoughts and see that they are not as solid and real as we usually think they are.

15. Breathing space

Practising breathing

We've been exploring mindfulness in different forms, and tasting a variety of practices. But if you'd like to deepen your experience, it's good to settle on one practice and try it regularly for a period of time. That way you can become familiar with the practice, and at the same time discover that it is different every time; each moment is unique, and therefore each session is unique.

Mindfulness courses like MBSR and MBCT normally begin with practices which focus on body sensations – the body scan and mindful movement. Through this approach, participants can develop their experience of being more grounded in the body, more fully embodied. These exercises are usually done with guidance from a teacher (in a classroom, or at home on audio), and sessions usually last about 30 minutes or more.

If you're just starting out on your own without a class, you may find that mindfulness of breathing is the simplest technique for you to develop first as a regular practice. You can do it on your own without audio or other guidance, and you can do it for any length of time and in almost any location. It helps if you can set aside at least 5–10 minutes each day for this practice, perhaps building up to 20–30 minutes as you feel comfortable.

As you make a connection with the mindful breathing practice, you are linking in with one of the oldest and most prevalent forms of meditation in the world. It is simple to explain, but seasoned meditators practise it for decades and still find something new to explore. You're tuning in to the act which keeps you alive, and developing an anchor for your awareness which is available to you at any moment, until the day you take your last breath.

Mindfulness of breathing: this week

See if you can practise mindfulness of breathing every day for the next week (see Chapter 5 for instructions). You could aim to practise for 5–10 minutes, or longer if you feel inspired. You may find it helpful to set a timer so you don't have to keep looking at your watch. If you don't think you have enough time one day, see if you can sit down for just 2 minutes!

Keep a diary and make a short note – even just a word or phrase – about what you notice during the practice each time. If you're finding it difficult, look at Chapter 16, where we discuss different kinds of challenges and how to work with them.

Monday	
Tuesday	
Wednesday	
Thursday	
Friday	
Saturday	
Sunday	

Three-step breathing space

As well as setting aside formal time for mindfulness of breathing, you can also take a 'breathing space' at any time in your day. This is a way to step out of automatic pilot and reconnect with the present moment.

We already introduced a short breathing space in Chapter 5, which we called a pause. We just stopped for a moment and took a few conscious breaths, and then moved on.

The three-step breathing space is an extension of this pause, taking a bit more time and bringing more awareness into the process. It is sometimes called the three-minute breathing space, but it doesn't have to be three minutes – it could be 30 seconds, a minute, or longer. It's a way to bring formal meditation practice into everyday life.

TRY IT NOW!

Three-step breathing space

Take a moment to come into an upright posture – sitting or standing, eyes open or closed, as you wish. There are three parts to the instructions.

Part 1: awareness

Ask yourself: 'What's happening in this moment for me? What thoughts, emotions and body sensations am I experiencing right now?' Don't start analysing in a big way – just feel in your body what's going on, and be present. See if you can acknowledge and accept any difficult feelings just as they are, even if they're unwanted.

Part 2: breathing

Now bring your attention to your breath. Gently direct your full focus to the physical sensations of breathing. Experience each in-breath and each out-breath. Let the breath help you to focus your awareness and bring you into the present.

Part 3: expanding

Expand your awareness around the breath to the sense of your whole body, as if your whole body is breathing. Have a sense of the space your body takes up, and the space around you too – your environment. Let your awareness include any sensations you are feeling, even if they're difficult. Hold everything in this wider space of your awareness.

See if you can let this sense of space and awareness be with you as you continue your day.

This is a version of a very commonly-used mindfulness exercise which was originally published in *Mindfulness-Based Cognitive Therapy for Depression* by Zindel V. Segal, J. Mark G. Williams and John D. Teasdale.

That sequence of instructions is like an hourglass – a wide focus, followed by a narrow focus, followed by a wide focus.

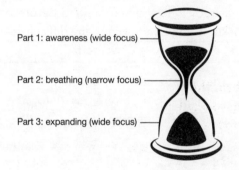

Part 1: awareness (wide focus)

Part 2: breathing (narrow focus)

Part 3: expanding (wide focus)

You can do this breathing space exercise wherever you have a few moments – sitting on a train, standing in a queue or waiting for the kettle to boil. As you become familiar with it, you can use this practice during stressful situations. At first though, it's good to practise regularly at more predictable times, so you can get used to it. Then it will be a tool that's available to you when you need to create space in moments of stress.

Breathing space: out and about

Pick an activity you do regularly a few times a day – it could be waiting for a bus, making coffee, or waiting for your computer to start up. Use this as a reminder to practise the three-step breathing space. See if you can do it a few times a day until it becomes familiar to you.

Your reminder:

The breath can become a powerful tool for bringing your awareness into the present moment. To develop this:

- Set aside formal time to practise mindfulness of breathing

- See how you can bring the 'breathing space' into your daily activities.

16. Challenges

Mindfulness practice sounds simple. Just sit down and follow your breath, or lie down and pay attention to different parts of the body – how hard can that be? But for most of us, these seemingly simple practices are surprisingly difficult. Chances are that when you first begin, you will think you are a bad meditator. You may think that everyone else can do it except you. Wrong! We all have challenges which come up in our practice. We get bored, frustrated, irritated, sleepy, angry … and this is all a natural part of the process.

If you find mindfulness difficult, don't be discouraged. For thousands of years meditators have been experiencing similar obstacles, and have written encouragement, suggestions and 'antidotes'. No matter how difficult our experiences, there are ways to work with the problems and learn from them. Often facing up to these challenges is the way we learn the most about ourselves and the patterns of our minds. As we see our habits more clearly, we can gradually open up to fresh ways of experiencing the world.

 Aaron
Aaron is an actor and writer in his 30s.

When you start meditating, at first you think it's brilliant because it calms you down. Then you can come to this place where you suddenly realize how noisy your brain is – you see all your thoughts and your emotions. Your watcher becomes stronger, and it can be a bit overwhelming. The noise in your head feels like a waterfall. The best advice I had is, just keep going, stay with it. You can find every little excuse not to – 'What shall I have for lunch?'... 'I've got to go and call my dad'... but just stay with it.

Restlessness

It's very common to feel restless when we first start to meditate. You feel twitchy, you want to get up and move, even run right out of the door. You may feel like a child who's been told to sit still and wants to rebel.

See if you can just be with this restless feeling, without acting on it. Where do you feel the restlessness in your body? Is there a sensation in the legs, arms or hands of wanting to move? Is there an itchiness, shakiness, vibration, or tension somewhere? Can you be curious about this restless energy and how it manifests in your body?

Sleepiness

We often find when we meditate that we are much more tired than we realized. We start the practice and are overcome by drowsiness, even drifting into sleep. Don't give yourself a hard time about it. Instead of setting up a feeling of struggle, see if you can practise an attitude of non-judgement, accepting the sleepiness as how things are in this moment.

You can encourage a greater sense of wakefulness by making sure you have an upright posture, with your spine tall and self-supporting. Feel the solid connection of your feet to the floor and your weight on the cushion or chair. If you find that sleepiness is your dominant challenge, try practising at a different time of day. It may also be that your body is sending you a message that you need more sleep!

Boredom

Our lives are normally so full of entertainment – we can hardly take a five-minute train journey without turning on the ipod, texting a friend or reading a newspaper. No wonder, when we take all this away, it can seem very boring. This boredom can manifest as restlessness, feeling twitchy and wanting to move; or as a dull, flat sort of boredom, just spacing out and losing interest.

When you notice boredom, see if you can rekindle your natural inquisitiveness. For example, can you be more curious about the object of meditation? If you're working with mindfulness of breath, are you taking for granted that each breath is the same? (*'Yeah, breath, I know what that is already, nothing interesting about breath.'*) See if you can approach each breath as something unique, paying attention to the texture and other qualities of the breath, as listed in Chapter 5. Remember there is no special way to breathe; you are simply bringing curiosity to this breath, in this moment.

You can also direct your curiosity to the feeling of boredom itself. How does your body feel when you are bored? Are there any physical signs and sensations of boredom? Are there other emotions under the boredom? For example, sometimes 'boredom' is covering up things we don't want to feel, such as fear or sadness. See if you can be gently curious about what's really here, rather than taking your boredom at face value. As you develop this curiosity, you may find that the practice is much richer and more interesting than you realized.

Pain and discomfort

Back pain, stiff shoulders, sore knees, ankles falling asleep – all manner of aches and pains can arise during your practice. Sometimes they become so distracting you can think of nothing else.

One possibility is that you actually need to change your posture – perhaps the height of your seat is wrong for you, or you're holding your arms in a way that puts tension in your shoulders. If this is the case, see if you can make the changes mindfully, rather than just shifting around. Make a decision to move, then move with awareness, and tune in to how the change affects your body sensations.

If the discomfort is not something you can alleviate, another option – which takes some courage – is to bring your awareness right up close to the discomfort, and kindly investigate what is here. Is it sharp or dull, constant or changing? See Chapter 13 for an exercise on working with difficult sensations. The pain may not go away, but you can alter your relationship with it – instead of fighting with it, you can start to make some sort of friendship with it, or at least a more peaceful co-existence. You may notice how your struggle with the discomfort creates extra layers of pain, and explore if it's possible to soften in those places of bracing and resistance.

Laziness

This is a challenge which can keep us from even sitting down to meditate. We intend to get up early, but we hit the snooze button. We plan to meditate after supper, but we end up watching TV. We set aside time for mindfulness but we get caught up in emails. We can find a lot of other activities we need to do instead of practising. Sometimes this looks like busyness but it can simply be another form of laziness. (There may also be other ingredients like fear which are involved here, so see if you can be gently curious about why you're finding it so hard to get round to your practice.) And then sometimes when we *do* sit down to practise, we may find that we let ourselves space out, without investing much effort into the session.

When this happens, there's no need to be hard on ourselves – we can just make a fresh start, and reconnect with our inspiration to practise. Take a moment to think about why you are doing this. Remember what inspired you to try this, and what you would like to get from it. You could look again at the intention you wrote down in Chapter 3.

A fresh sense of inspiration can help to overcome our natural procrastination and avoidance tactics.

Doubt

'What am I doing here? This is a waste of time. I'm hopeless at this. I'm doing it wrong. I'm not getting anything from this.' You're likely to have all kinds of doubts, whether about mindfulness as an approach, or about your own ability to practise it.

If doubts arise during your practice, see if you can recognize that they are thoughts just like any others. Instead of buying into them, recognize them as distractions from the practice you have committed yourself to doing in this moment. See if you can let them go, returning your focus to the object of meditation.

Make a decision to 'suspend your disbelief' for this time while you are practising. You've decided to give mindfulness a go, and you know that it's not a quick fix, and that there will be challenges. So, see if you can drop the commentating voice which constantly judges things to be good or bad, useful or without use – just get on with doing the practice right now as best you can!

Sadness

We're used to thinking of sadness as a problem. When someone asks how you are, you are supposed to smile and say 'fine'. But it's part of life to feel sad; we live in a world where things change, where friends and family get ill, where partners leave us, and where ultimately we all die! To feel sadness is very human. Even our most joyful moments can contain sadness, as we know that nothing can last forever. When we hear a piece of music or see a sunset that is so beautiful it makes us want to cry, we may not be sure if it's joy or sadness, as the two feelings are so intertwined.

Often we armour ourselves against feeling sadness, closing off our hearts from the rawness of this emotion. In meditation we can gently let ourselves be more open to the experience of sadness. Chögyam Trungpa writes about 'the genuine heart of sadness' which comes from allowing ourselves to be tender and open. This is part of what it means to be more fully human, more awake and alive.

You can be gentle with yourself in this process of allowing in feelings that you might normally bury. But don't feel that sadness is a problem – it is a sign that you are opening up and softening. Being willing to experience your own sadness also helps you to be able to be with the sadness of others, and not to require the people in your life to be constantly jolly and 'fine'.

SPEAKING FROM EXPERIENCE

Aaron

If you're the kind of person who has trouble growing up, I think meditation really helps turn you into an adult. Being an adult is about connecting with the world and taking responsibility for stuff. That means feeling and being open to things. And that's what meditation helps you to do – it helps you have the presence and the ability to stay open in difficult situations, situations of suffering. It has slowly changed me and allowed me to be present. When friends' parents have died or something like that, I'm much more able to stay present and not just run away and eat pizza and play computer games which is my general survival tactic.

Emotions

Sometimes you may be surprised by what arises when you're meditating. You're just sitting there minding your own business and *whoosh*; you are swept up in a strong emotion such as anger, lust, desire, grief, or jealousy. There may be a difficult situation in your life right now which is an obvious cause, or it may be an old feeling which seems to well up out of nowhere.

When you feel a strong emotion like this, see if you can reconnect as fully as possible with your sense of being present in your body. Feel your feet on the ground, and your bum on the seat. You could have a sense that the weight of your body tethers you to the earth, and keeps you from being swept away by the force of the emotion. You can also reconnect with the texture of your breath, and its rhythmic movement.

Then see if you can be curious about the nature and quality of the emotion. When you feel this anger or jealousy, are there sensations anywhere in the body which accompany it? Perhaps a resistance or bracing in the torso somewhere; a shakiness in the chest, a tightness in the throat, or a clenching in the belly?

Normally when we feel an emotion we are very caught up in the story we are telling ourselves – 'Then I did this, and then she said that, and then you did this.' See if you can let go of the storyline and feel the raw energy of the emotion. Does it have a location in the body? Does it have a texture, a shape?

Don't worry if this feels impossible – it's not an easy practice to drop our 'thinking' about a particular situation, and be present with the energy of the 'feeling'. But just by sitting there on your cushion or chair, experiencing your anger without shouting or throwing things, chances are you are doing something more valuable than you realize. So often we act out strong emotions, or we repress and bury them. Here you are allowing them to be there, letting them unfold in their own way. You may find that they are less solid than they seemed, and that by giving space to the emotions you make them more able to dissipate, or at least to flow and move through you rather than holding you in a fixed and stony grip.

Emotions, like thoughts and sensations, are changing all the time. Instead of fighting them, or trying to hold on to them, we can let them move through us like the changing weather. As always, be gentle in this process, and if it all feels overwhelming, come back to the movement of your breath, or whatever focus you are working with, as an anchor for your awareness.

Fear

Fear may not always be instantly recognizable as fear. You may find yourself fidgety, restless; maybe there is a buzz of adrenaline, like when you've had too much coffee; or feelings of doubt and irritation about what on earth you are doing here. If we can be gently curious, we will often find that beneath other feelings like impatience or boredom, there is fear. We are scared of this silence and space. We are scared of sitting here so intimately with ourselves, with nothing to entertain or distract us. It may feel like a great void, with nothing to hang on to.

The good news is that great meditation teachers see this fear as something extremely important and valuable. Chögyam Trungpa writes that 'because we possess such fear, we are also potentially entitled to experience fearlessness. True fearlessness is not the reduction of fear, but going beyond fear.' We can teach ourselves to recognize fear, and to let ourselves feel it. Through this practice, the fear lessens its unconscious power over us, and we are able to open up to the world and to aspects of our experience we may have been shutting down.

Our natural instinct is to push fear away, or deny it, but that only increases its hold on us. As with other experiences, mindfulness encourages us to be curious about it – to let ourselves feel its energy. We can do this by noticing what is going on in the body. Where is the fear located? Are there body sensations? See if you can allow the sensations of fear, without feeling you need to change anything. Remember you can 'breathe in' to any sensations which are difficult.

'Feel the fear and do it anyway', as Susan Jeffers' popular book title puts it. But as with everything in mindfulness practice, we need to do this gently. If you experience fear that feels overwhelming, don't feel you have to barge straight into it. Let yourself come up to the edges of it, and explore it in your own time. Be kind to yourself. If things feel unmanageable, you can return your attention to a safe haven such as your breath or your body.

Don't feel you need to identify and label your fear as being 'about' anything in particular. Meditation practice may bring up some of our most basic, nameless fears such as the fear of non-existence. The busyness of our daily activity is constantly confirming us in how we define ourselves. When we stop that activity or slow it down, we may be frightened of somehow losing ourselves, of no longer existing. At the bottom may even be the fear of death itself – the final non-existing – which we rarely confront. But there is no need to get into too much analysis. Instead, mindfulness practice encourages us to accept the fear as a natural part of being alive, and to let it be here.

If you have started mindfulness practice, even a little, it's worth congratulating yourself on your own bravery.

It takes courage to be still with nothing but yourself and whatever emotions and fears may arise. You may think of bravery as diving off a high board or going into battle or making a speech. But possibly one of the bravest acts we can do is to sit down on our bottoms and 'do nothing'. Each of these small acts of bravery may slowly help us to be more courageous in our interactions with the world as we go through our lives.

- Real fearlessness is not being without fear, but 'going beyond' fear by acknowledging its presence

- When you notice fear coming up, see if you can tune in to any physical sensations with gentle awareness – and allow them to be here.

Sitting meditation: working with challenges

- Practise mindfulness of breathing for 5 to 10 minutes. Or if you prefer, you could work with another focus such as sounds.

- During this practice, notice if there is a tendency towards one or more of the experiences described in this chapter – and if so which ones.

- At the end of the practice, take a moment to reflect on what was your major challenge. Are you tending to drift off into sleep? Do you feel restless or full of anger?

- Is this a common experience for you, or is it particular to this session? What other difficulties have you encountered in your practice so far?

- Read again about the challenges which feel most familiar to you, and the suggestions for how to work with them. See if you can put this into practice the next time you meditate.

- If you like you could even repeat this exercise right now and try out the suggestions for how to work with whichever challenge is most dominant in your practice.

Your biggest challenge(s) when you practise:

_____

_____

If you don't feel you have any particular challenges that's fine! You can return to this chapter at any point when you are finding the practices difficult.

See if you can begin to train your mind to be aware of the state it is in. You can start to develop a vigilance about what arises. You can be gently curious about any states of mind you are experiencing, and what lies underneath them. Whatever the challenge, the first step is being clear about what is going on – then you can see how best to work with it.

17. Kindness

Marion
Since I started practising mindfulness, a few people have commented that they're finding me very gentle. The more I spend time coming up close to who I am, the more I think it's changed the way I look at other people. It's not that I would have said I wasn't an empathetic person before, but I think that my empathy is more authentic now. I'm so aware of the hidden emotions in myself behind each consciously experienced emotion. I also think I'm getting a bit gentler in terms of my judgements of other people – I'm seeing other people as more complex groupings of emotions. It's all stuff that I knew intellectually before, but there's a difference between talking about something intellectually and really experiencing it.

Most of us are very hard on ourselves. As we've noticed already in our practice, no matter how confident we may seem, we often have an internal voice which is critical and hard to please. If we are unforgiving to ourselves, we may find we are also hard on other people. Likewise, the more we can be kind to ourselves, the more genuine kindness we can show to others.

We might think that kindness is a personality trait which we either have or don't have – we all know people who seem to be naturally sweet and generous, and we may think 'that's not me'. We may even pride ourselves on being a bit spiky, a bit tough. But we all know there have been times when we've made ourselves and others unhappy by being irritable, angry or sullen in a situation where we could have been more generous and forgiving. Mindfulness practice shows us that we all have an innate capacity for kindness; we just need to create the right conditions for it to flourish and flow. This is not a one-shot deal, but a lifelong process of opening up to ourselves and other people, as we are, with all our quirks and imperfections.

The writer and teacher Pema Chödrön tells a story in *Taking the Leap* which she says was circulating after the September 2001 bombings in New York. A native American grandfather was trying to explain the existence of violence and cruelty to his grandson. He said it was like he had two wolves fighting in his heart: one angry and one kind. The grandson asked who would win this fight between the wolves, and the grandfather answered 'The one I choose to feed'. Pema encourages us to recognize that it's up to us, in each moment, to choose whether to 'feed the right wolf'.

In mindfulness training, we can practise 'feeding the right wolf' by paying attention to the tone of our inner voice. As we've discussed throughout this book, no matter what formal practice we are doing, we can develop a tone of greater kindness in the way that we bring ourselves back to the focus of meditation each time. When you find yourself getting frustrated with the busyness of your mind, or other experiences, see if you can develop gentleness and humour in the way you usher your mind back to its focus, like a dog-lover herding a wayward puppy. This is an important retraining of your internal voice which will slowly seep into the rest of your life.

You can also work more directly with practices which cultivate your compassion for yourself and others. These practices are known in Buddhism as 'maitri' practices, from the Sanskrit word *maitri* which can be translated as compassion, friendliness or loving kindness. Do take these practices gently – they can sometimes bring up a lot of emotions. Or you may feel the opposite: a bit of a blank. Don't worry if you don't feel the words you are saying, just try it out as an experiment without expecting to feel anything in particular.

It's good to always 'sandwich' a practice like this with simple mindfulness of breath at the beginning and end. We start with awareness of breath and body to ground ourselves and create a sense of stability within which the loving kindness practice can take place. If you feel overwhelmed at any point, just come back to your breath and let yourself be steadied and soothed by its natural rhythm.

Loving kindness meditation

1. **Mindfulness of breath.** Sit in an upright position, feel your connection to the ground, and practise a few minutes of mindfulness of breath. When your mind feels somewhat steady, you can begin the loving kindness practice.

2. **Yourself.** Now bring an image of yourself to mind, as if you could see yourself standing right in front of you. Have a sense of sending yourself good wishes, warmth and kindness. You could imagine giving yourself a warm blanket, a cup of tea, or whatever would make you feel happy and loved. You can say to yourself, either in these words, or your own words:

May I be safe
May I be happy
May I be free from suffering
May I be at ease

Spend a few minutes feeling the essence of these words, and generating these feelings of loving kindness for yourself. You may find this challenging and emotional, or awkward and artificial – don't worry, just have a go and see what it feels like. See if you can bring kindness and gentleness to whatever arises for you. You are welcome to stay with generating kindness for yourself for the rest of the practice, as this is usually the area we need to work with most. Remember to return to mindfulness of breath for the last few minutes of the meditation.

3. **A person you love.** If you'd like to carry on, now let this image of yourself fade, and bring to mind someone you find easy to love and wish well for. It could be a child, friend or relative, but make it someone for whom your feelings are not too complicated; it could even be a dog or cat. Visualize this person or creature in front of you, send them feelings of compassion and kindness, and again say these words, or just feel the essence of them: 'May they be safe, may they be happy, may they be free from suffering, may they be at ease.' Spend a few minutes visualizing this person you love and generating good wishes for their happiness.

4. **A neutral person.** Now let that person fade in your mind's eye, and bring to mind somebody neutral; someone you don't know very well, and don't have strong feelings for or against. It could be a neighbour, or someone who works in the shop where you buy your newspaper. Bring their image in front of you, and see what it's like to generate the same feelings of wishing them well. Repeat the process from step 3 with this

153

neutral person in front of you. Feel free to stop after this stage and return to mindfulness of breath.

5. **A difficult person.** If you'd like to continue, let this neutral person fade and now bring to mind someone who is a bit difficult in your life. Don't pick the *most* difficult person, but perhaps someone you have a slightly challenging relationship with, and may find it hard to wish well for. Picture this person in front of you and repeat the same process. See what it feels like to generate warmth and compassion for this person.

6. **All four people.** Now let this person fade, and bring all four of the people in front of you, in your mind's eye: yourself, the person you love easily, the neutral person and the difficult person. See how it feels to send out good wishes and compassion to all of these people equally, saying to yourself 'May we be safe, may we be happy, may we be free from suffering, may we be at ease.' Is it possible to send out this loving kindness with equanimity for all of these people, yourself included?

7. **All beings.** If it feels right for you, as a final stage you can let these four people fade into the background, and imagine yourself extending these feelings of kindness beyond this immediate circle, out into the neighbourhood and the city – to all the people you know and don't know. Expand as far as your imagination will let

you, out to the country, the globe – to people suffering from war and natural disasters, illness and unhappiness. Send out these wishes for all people and beings: 'May we be safe … may we be at ease.'

Then let go of this contemplation, and rest for a few moments noticing any sensations in the body. How does it feel when you've been generating these feelings of compassion and kindness?

8. **Mindfulness of breath.** Return your awareness to the movement of your breath. Spend a few minutes re-grounding yourself in the physical sensations of your breath moving in your body.

As we mentioned above, the loving kindness practice can be challenging and emotional. Some of us find it hard to wish kindness for ourselves – maybe it feels selfish. Or we may find it too difficult to generate good wishes for the neutral and difficult people. If this practice feels too uncomfortable, don't force it; feel free to come back to explore it again at some other time.

You may like to write down something about your experience of this practice:

_____

_____

_____

Looking after yourself

As you start to bring mindfulness into your daily activities, you could become more aware of how you spend your time. Are you showing kindness to yourself in your daily life? How often do you sit too long at the computer without a screen break, as if in a hypnotic trance? How often do you forget to eat properly, or to go outside on a sunny day? We can all get caught up in activities and habits which deplete our energy, and neglect to do the things which we know are nourishing.

When we become more mindful, we can notice if we're not looking after ourselves properly, and show some greater kindness to ourselves during the course of our day. There's an exercise used in MBCT which can help us to see this more clearly. (The original version of this exercise is published in *Mindfulness-Based Cognitive Therapy for Depression* by Zindel V. Segal, J. Mark G. Williams and John D. Teasdale.)

Mindfulness of your day

- Make a list of the things you do in a typical day. If you don't have a typical day, pick any recent day. Write the list in some detail, e.g. *wake up, make tea, have a shower, listen to the news, eat breakfast,* and so on.

- When you're finished, look at the list and put a letter beside each activity:

  N = Nourishing: things which increase your energy, nourish you, help you feel awake and alive
  D = Depleting: things which drain your energy, deplete you, make you feel less awake and alive.

  (There may be some activities which can be either, so it's fine to put both.)

- Now have a good look at your list and notice what seems interesting, or surprising. Are there a lot of nourishing activities, or more draining ones? Are there some things which can be either, depending on the attitude you bring to them – if so, what makes the difference? Do you find it difficult to be kind to yourself and do the things that you know are energizing and nourishing?

- Reflect on your list and see if there is anything you could change. There may be some things you don't have control over, but is there a way you could do more of the nourishing activities and fewer of the depleting ones? What would those be? Make a note of one or two things you would like to change:

_____

_____

One way we can start to be more kind to ourselves is to keep creating little spaces in our day, where we can notice what we're doing, and change direction if we need to. We began this process with the short 'pause' in Chapter 4, and continued this with the 3-step 'breathing space' in Chapter 15. Now we can revisit the breathing space, adding a few more details about how we can use it in times of stress or busyness.

Breathing space: creating a choice

If you are very busy or stressed, you may find it's hard to do even such a short practice without getting distracted. It can help to talk yourself through the process, using your internal commentator as a way of directing your focus. Begin with an awake and dignified posture – sitting or standing.

Part 1: awareness

Ask yourself: 'What's happening for me right now?' It may help to say to yourself 'my stomach is clenched', or 'I'm feeling really irritated', or 'I'm worrying that I can't do this job on time'. Let yourself acknowledge any difficult feelings and allow them to be here.

Part 2: breathing

Bring your full attention to a very specific focus: the movement of your breath. It may help to say to yourself 'breathing in, breathing out' – or even to count the breaths up to 5 or 10. Often when we're stressed our breath gets shallow, so you may also find it helpful to see if you can let your belly relax and feel the movement of your breath down in the belly area.

Part 3: expanding

Expand your awareness so that as well as feeling the sensations of breathing, you are also aware of your body as a whole, including any sensations in it. Allow any difficult feelings to be here too – you could say to yourself, 'It's ok to feel this way.' Have a sense of your body and the space around you too. See if you can allow this sense of space to be with you as you move back into your day.

And what next?

As you finish your breathing space, ask yourself – what's the best thing for me to do in this moment? How can I look after myself? It could be that you need to carry on with whatever you were doing, and if that's the case, can you do it with mindfulness, being present? Or is this the moment to do something nourishing for yourself? Perhaps make a cup of tea, get some fresh air, or talk to a friend? Instead of getting stuck on automatic pilot, use the breathing space as a moment to have a choice about what to do next, and to be kind to yourself.

This exercise is adapted from one in *Mindfulness-Based Cognitive Therapy for Depression* by Zindel V. Segal, J. Mark G. Williams and John D. Teasdale.

Mindfulness helps you to develop a kindness and friendliness to yourself which will naturally start to extend to other people. This can happen:

- Through any of the formal mindfulness practices, as you start to let go of judging yourself, and let things be as they are

- Through loving kindness practices where you can explore what it's like to generate warm feelings for yourself and others

- Through being mindful of your activities and doing things which energize and nourish you during the day.

18. Slowing down

It's possible to be mindful at any speed – you can be sure an Olympic sprinter is completely focused and present for those 10 seconds it takes to run the 100 metres. We can be mindful when we're running, skiing, cycling or salsa dancing, and we can enjoy the feeling of speed in its right place. But we all know there are times when speed becomes mindless, and when 21st-century life seems to be one big race. We find we're unable to appreciate life because we're rushing through it, with one eye always on the clock.

Since the Industrial Revolution, we've been living by the creed that faster is better, with industry and business leading the way. But in recent years, an alternative viewpoint has been developing in the form of the 'slow movement' – not one organization, but a number of different groups and advocates suggesting it's time for a cultural shift. Journalist Carl Honoré became a spokesperson for slowing down after an epiphany when he found himself speed-reading bedtime stories to his two-year-old son. His book *In Praise of Slow* is not about living life at a snail's pace, but finding the right speed for everything we do: what musicians call the *tempo giusto*.

The slow philosophy is essentially about bringing mindfulness into our daily life – being present to what's going on in each moment, rather than rushing through doing too much at once, and always thinking of the next task. Evidence shows that working excessive hours and not taking breaks does not actually make us more productive – billions are lost each year in the costs of work-related stress. By allowing more space in your day, and varying the pace, you can be more creative and productive, as well as having time to enjoy life more.

This chapter draws on the ideas of Slow Down London, a group (including this author) which has been working on ways to encourage a saner pace of life in one of the world's big cities.

Notice your speed

- For the next few days, see if you can be more aware of your pace at different times during the day. Are you going fast or slowly? Are you at the right speed for the task you are doing in this moment? Sometimes we do need to hurry, but check – if you are rushing, do you need to be?

- It may be helpful to pick one activity or signal which you use as a reminder to do a speed check. It could be each time the phone rings, each time you boil the kettle, each time you wash your hands. This is just like the 'pause' we've already been practising, but you could also bring awareness to the pace you're going at, and notice if it's time to slow down or take a break.

- Write down your signal here:

_____

- Don't feel you need to make a judgement or feel bad about your speed – just train yourself to notice. If you find you have an internal speed demon, see if you can develop a sense of kindness and humour towards it!

One thing at a time

As we try to do everything faster, we're meant to be proud of our ability to multi-task. Our electronic technology seems to encourage doing 5 or 10 things at once: juggling email, web searching, instant messaging, writing documents, taking phone calls, texting, listening to music, watching a video and eating a sandwich at our desk.

But research has started to show that this constant switching of attention from one task to another is actually hugely counter-productive. Each time we let ourselves be distracted from working on a task to answer an email, it takes time and energy to switch focus, and then to return our attention to the original task. One study at the University of London in 2005 found that workers distracted by email and phone calls suffer a fall in IQ more than twice that found in marijuana smokers! Another American study in 2007 claimed that extreme multi-tasking costs the US economy $650 billion a year in lost productivity.

Apart from the fact that we actually get less done, multi-tasking can leave us feeling jittery, unfocused and exhausted. By contrast, doing one task at a time, mindfully, can be more satisfying and less depleting of our energy. Uni-tasking: it's the new multi-tasking! As Lord Chesterfield wrote in the 1740s:

> 'There is time enough for everything in the course of the day, if you do but one thing at once, but there is not time enough in the year, if you will do two things at a time ... The steady and undissipated attention to one object, is a sure mark of a superior genius; as hurry, bustle, and agitation are the never-failing symptoms of a weak and frivolous mind.'

Uni-tasking

This week, practise doing one thing at a time, especially in the way you use technology.

- Next time you sit down at your computer, make a pact with yourself to do one thing at a time. Switch your email off, and check it once an hour, or less if that's practical. If you're working on a task, turn off other distractions like instant messaging and Facebook.

- If you want to listen to radio or watch TV, really listen or watch rather than doing other things at the same time.

- When you use your phone, see if you can give the other person your full attention for the duration of the call.

- While you are eating, set aside other activities, and just eat.

Slow activities

The word 'slow' has been adopted in a number of fields as a byword for paying more attention to quality and substance, as opposed to fast, take-away, throw-away culture. Slow Food is a growing movement which arose in Italy, and which supports traditional cuisine and regional products. Slow Travel encourages taking the train, bus or boat instead of flying, and enjoying the journey not just the destination. Slow Cities (or *Cittaslow*) is a network which celebrates the special qualities of each town, and resists homogenization. The slow philosophy has a lot in common with environmentalism, encouraging us to be more aware of the ecological and social impact of wanting everything to be fast and convenient.

Practising mindfulness doesn't mean you have to sign up to any of these slow movements, but you may find some ideas here that are worth exploring. For example, there may be days when a quick take-away is in order, but sometimes you might find it satisfying to visit the local farmers' market and take time to cook a meal, or to engage in a slow, traditional activity which uses your hands, such as painting, knitting, baking, gardening or carpentry. Many of us spend our days in our heads – thinking through problems, sitting at computers, attending meetings. There is something about doing things with our hands which can bring us into the present moment. It feels soothing and refreshing after a day of mental activity, and we feel once again embodied.

Slow activity

This week, find one activity which helps you slow down and be mindful – hopefully something which you also enjoy! Here are some ideas, but you may have others. If you already do some of these things, you could pick something new, or bring the activity into your life at a different time. For example, if you normally garden at the weekend, could you head outside on a weekday evening after work instead of flopping in front of the TV?

- Cook a meal from scratch, being mindful of the whole process, from shopping to chopping vegetables to eating.

- Write a letter. Find a nice pen and stationery, if you can, or just use what's to hand. Sit down and write to a friend or family member. It doesn't matter what you write. Post it and imagine their surprise. When was the last time you wrote or received a letter that wasn't business mail or a bill?

- Do something with your hands: digging, painting, knitting, playing an instrument or building some shelves. If you have children, try playing with their plasticine or making a castle with Lego. (Or feel free to go out and buy something playful and childish for yourself!)

- Take a walk somewhere different. Look up and around. Be like a tourist in your own city, noticing the cafés, churches, shops, architecture and people.

- Write down your slow activity:

_____

_____

_____

 Mindfulness doesn't mean doing everything at a snail's pace, but you may feel less exhausted and depleted if you can consciously:

- Notice your speed

- Do one thing at a time

- Make space for some activities you enjoy which can help you to slow down and be mindful.

19. Me

True happiness, we are told, consists in getting out of one's self; but the point is not only to get out – you must stay out; and to stay out you must have some absorbing errand.

Henry James

What is your first thought when you get up in the morning? The meditation master Sakyong Mipham suggests it is likely to be a version of 'What about me? Will I get what I want today?' This is a mantra that we learn to recite subconsciously throughout our day.

This 'What about me?' mantra doesn't actually make us happy, because it's based on a false version of reality. We see ourselves as the centre of the universe, and we are constantly disappointed and resentful that the universe doesn't give us exactly what we want. At the times when we stop worrying about getting what we want and are able to think of the bigger picture – including the needs of other people – we may paradoxically feel more cheerful.

This doesn't mean that we can't look after ourselves properly, or that it's selfish to have a nice hot bath or take a weekend break. Even if we are not the centre of the universe in the way we imagined it, we are still walking around with a mind and body which are unique and worth taking care of. As we discussed in Chapter 17, we can cultivate a kindness to both ourselves and other people.

However, a lot of what we do for ourselves is not always making us happier. We try to get what we think will make us feel happy and safe: the new job, the nice flat, the beautiful partner. But we are never satisfied and always wanting something else.

As we practise mindfulness, we may start to notice how, by trying to protect this 'me', we often isolate ourselves from others, and cut ourselves off from our own experience. We create an idea of how things should be, and then we get stuck with our version of things and miss something much more interesting. We try to make ourselves a little nest which feels safe, but it starts to get airless and claustrophobic. We re-run the same old stories, and replay the same old scenarios. But because it feels familiar, we're scared to come out.

It's like we're stuck in a motel room under a smelly old duvet, eating stale crisps and watching bad reality TV. We've pulled all the curtains closed and there's no light. But then we open the curtains a crack, and then the window. We discover there's a fresh breeze blowing and warm sea air. Slowly we start to open up all the windows until sunlight and fresh air come flooding in. Eventually, we might even take down all the walls, and find we're standing under a huge sky.

In our mindfulness practice we can start to see our habitual patterns of thought and behaviour more clearly. We can let in some fresh air and discover that there's a whole big world out there, and we don't always have to relate to it and react to it in the same old ways – and that shockingly, mercifully, we are not at the centre of it! There are lots of other 'me's walking around out there too. Of course we know this, but do we *really* know it?

Many 'me's

- Sit in a place where other people come and go – it could be a café, a bus or train, or a waiting room.

- Watch the people as if you are a novelist or film director who wants to include them as characters, and needs to understand them. Use your imagination. What kind of a day are they having? What is going on in their minds? What kind of thoughts and emotions are they experiencing?

- Pay special attention to the people you don't find immediately interesting or attractive. Why does that guy look so sullen and sour? What might be the reason for his unhappiness – perhaps he's just lost his girlfriend, or had a fight with his father? Or maybe he missed his train and is late for a meeting? Or his cheese sandwich was stale?

- If it feels right, you can also see what it's like to generate a sense of wishing them well, as in Chapter 17: 'May they be safe, may they be happy, may they be free from suffering, may they be at ease.' If that feels too much, just notice them with the awareness that, like you, each of these strangers has a whole world of thoughts and feelings going on inside.

---

20. Society

As mindfulness becomes more mainstream, people who have found it important in their own lives are naturally turning outwards and looking at how to bring it into their environment. How could we create a more mindful society – and what would that look like?

Some of the most exciting and successful projects have been focusing on how we can teach mindfulness skills from an early age. In schools in Vancouver, Canada, four- and five-year-old children begin their day with a few minutes of mindful breathing. They are taught how to calm themselves in moments of stress, and to listen to their emotions. They draw pictures of their brain, and talk about which parts are used in processing their emotional reactions.

In Tonbridge in the UK, school boys aged fourteen and fifteen take part in an eight-week mindfulness course designed specifically for adolescents. At the end, most of them say they are likely to keep using the techniques, especially as a way of coping with the pressures of exams and sports events.

Increasingly, mindfulness is being brought into education, healthcare, and many kinds of organizations and workplaces. Prisoners are being offered mindfulness training to help cope with their anxiety and frustration, and to develop 'emotional intelligence'. Lawyers are coming to mindfulness courses to improve their listening skills, clarify their thought processes, and deal with the intense emotions that can come up in the courtroom. Business people are learning mindful leadership as a foundation for better decision-making and communication. Parents are discussing ways to be more mindful in their family life and the way they interact with their children.

The way mindfulness is taught may have a different flavour and focus, according to the different needs of teenagers or lawyers or corporate leaders. But in the end it's all about learning to be more present and aware in an increasingly hectic world. And not only being present when we're sitting alone in meditation, but also when we are relating to other people.

Speaking and listening

We've talked about mindfulness as a way of allowing more space in our lives – creating gaps in our mental chatter and busyness. In our contact with other people we may also find there is normally not much sense of space. We react to each other in habitual ways; we jump in on what the other person is saying to make our own point, and we feel frustrated at speaking without being heard. We may find it hard even to hear ourselves – to hear the voice of what feels true rather than what we think we are supposed to say.

As you practise mindfulness, there's a natural spaciousness which may begin to seep into the way you are with other people. You can also practise intentionally bringing mindfulness into moments of communication.

- **Listening.** When you are listening, just listen, with your undivided attention – not planning what you are going to say next. If you drift off into other thoughts, gently bring yourself back to what the other person is saying.

- **Speaking.** When you are speaking, try allowing space – taking a 'pause' at any time. See if you can let whatever you say next emerge from that spaciousness rather than from a feeling of hurry and jumble.

- **Silences.** When no one is speaking, can you let it be that way? Are you always the one who jumps in to make conversation? If so, can you see what happens if you don't?

Let us not look east and west for materials of conversation, but rest in presence and unity. A just feeling will fast enough supply fuel for discourse, if speaking be more grateful than silence. When people come to see us, we foolishly prattle, lest we be inhospitable. But things said for conversation are chalk eggs. Don't say things. What you are stands over you the while, and thunders so that I cannot hear what you say to the contrary.

Ralph Waldo Emerson

Speaking and listening

This is an exercise to do with a friend or partner. It's just about bringing some of the same qualities you bring to your meditation practice into your interaction: being present, open and without judgement.

Pick a question you would both like to answer – it could be something you choose yourselves, or one of the following:

- What is difficult for you in your life right now?
- What does it feel like to be in your body?
- What do you long for in your life?
- What are you frightened of?
- What helps you to be present and what stops you from being present?

Choose one person to ask the question and listen to the answer; then reverse the roles. Take about five minutes for each speaker.

While you are the listener, don't speak – you don't even need to keep nodding and gesturing in response. Just listen with openness and without judgement.

When you are speaking, pause as often as you like and trust that words will emerge. (Or if you find you don't want to speak at all that would also be fine!)

When you've finished, take a few minutes to share what the experience was like. If it feels right you could repeat the exercise with another question, or even the same question again – you may be surprised to find something different emerging each time.

SPEAKING FROM EXPERIENCE

Isaac

The funny thing about mindfulness is that once you've had the taste of it, it's difficult to switch off. There's nothing more annoying than when you're in the middle of an argument and you know that at that point you're being really, really unreasonable! When you practise mindfulness there's an opportunity for you to either switch on and engage with other people, or switch off. The gift that mindfulness gives us is that when you make that decision to either switch on or switch off you are fully aware of it. You might deny it or make excuses, but you do know it!

21. Stillness

Peace and calm. We long for it – in our modern life it's a valuable commodity. We gaze at advertising hoardings showing a gleaming white beach and a turquoise sea. A woman in flowing white sits cross-legged with her eyes closed and a serene expression on her face. We want some of that! And so we spend lots of money on candles and aromatherapy oils, spa treatments, relaxation tapes, and *The Little Book of Calm*.

Not everyone believes in calm. Economist Todd Buchholz wrote a book called *Rush: Why You Need and Love the Rat Race*. He argues that we thrive on busyness, and that people who sit back and relax are miserable. We must all have friends or colleagues who'd agree with him – people who've built their lives on never stopping, and who work seven days a week; or else fill their weekends and evenings with activity which keeps them just as busy as on their working days. Or maybe we are those people ourselves!

Mindfulness is not necessarily about buying in to either of these caricatures. Yes, we do need to set aside time for 'doing nothing', or at least for doing the kind of nothing we cultivate in the meditation practices. But that doesn't mean we can't also thrive in a busy environment, and enjoy the buzz of the urban 'work hard, play hard' life. If we give ourselves times of space and stillness, this will help us to ride the waves of chaos when we need to.

Equanimity

The popular image of 'calm' can seem also to imply a person without emotions – serene and detached in all situations. But this is not the aim of mindfulness. We're not trying to get rid of all the fire and passion in life; to become boring, indifferent, or uncaring towards others. We're not denying our feelings – on the contrary, we can let ourselves feel the extraordinary power and energy of emotions. However, by being more aware and present to them, we don't let ourselves get swept around by them so much, and knocked into automatic, habitual reactions. It's like we're able to be at the eye of the storm, and not uprooted and blown around by the gale-force winds.

We could describe this quality as 'equanimity': a sense of inner balance or equilibrium which means we're not so easily blown off course by our reactions. Pema Chödrön says, 'To cultivate equanimity we practise catching ourselves when we feel attraction or aversion, before it hardens into grasping or negativity.' So it doesn't mean we don't feel, but we can create enough space to make a choice about what we do next, and how we act on those feelings.

Think of yourself as a surfer on the crest of a huge wave, or a rider on a bucking bronco. The surfer, or rider, is in relative stillness amidst a great whoosh of movement. How can you hold your balance in a similar way? This is one of our challenges in life: to have some sense of stillness and stability within our dynamic and constantly changing experience.

To be able to dance, as T. S. Eliot puts it, 'at the still point of the turning world'.

Meditation: stillness, stability, space

We've mentioned throughout this book that our meditation practice is not about trying to get calm, or aiming for any particular state of mind. This only sets up a struggle, wanting ourselves to be somehow different. If we do experience any feeling of increased calm, it's the kind of calm which comes from allowing things to be as they are, including sometimes accepting that at this moment we're not feeling very calm!

The natural world gives us some powerful images of what it might mean to embody stillness within flux and change, and stormy weather. Mountains and sky have already come up during the book as metaphors to use in our mindfulness practice, but now we can meditate or reflect on them a bit more. We can also bring these images to mind at any time in the middle of a chaotic day, and just for a moment have a sense of embodying these qualities ourselves.

Meditation: mountain

- Sit with good posture, and spend a few moments in mindfulness of your body and breath.

- Picture a mountain in front of you – either one you've seen, or one you can imagine. See the enormous size and majesty of the mountain, with its broad base in the earth, and its peak rising above the clouds.

- Now have a sense of bringing this mountain into your own body, with your base rooted in the earth, and your peak rising skyward. Feel the strength, stability and unwavering quality of the mountain. You can also feel your breath moving, like a gentle breeze.

- Imagine the seasons passing on the mountain: autumn, with its rain and winds; winter, bringing snow and sleet; spring, when the snows melt and flowers grow; summer, bringing the heat of sun onto the rocks. Take a few moments to imagine each season and the changing weather it brings. Throughout all these changes, the mountain remains present and unwavering.

- Spend some time feeling the mountain in yourself, a sense of stillness and rootedness through all the storms and difficulties of life. See if you can bring something of this mountain quality into the rest of your day.

Meditation: sky

- Settle into your meditation posture and practise mindfulness of breathing. Feel grounded in your body and breath. Let yourself be aware of any thoughts coming and going like clouds.

- Now picture a grey, rainy day. The clouds above you are thick and heavy, and fill the whole sky. They seem to be endless; they weigh you down.

- Then imagine yourself on a plane, taking off. The houses and cars are getting smaller below you. You enter the clouds, and everything is blank for a few moments. Then suddenly you burst into sunshine and blue sky. Picture the brightness of the blue, the whiteness of the clouds below you, and the relief – the blue sky has been here all along, and is always here.

- You can let the plane dissolve in your imagination and have a sense of just being up there above the clouds – perhaps you have a soft, firm white cloud as a seat. Let your mind open to the brilliance of the blue sky and the limitless space.

- Now rest your mind, with this feeling of space and sky. At the same time, you have a real sense of being in your body, feeling its weight sitting here, and your breath moving. When you're ready to finish, see if you can carry some of this feeling of space and vastness into the next moments of your day.

Tessa

When I was a child I was awed by the idea of space. I used to visit the city planetarium regularly, and watch light shows about the stars and galaxies. I remember making up a song on my guitar about my frustration that I would never know the answers to my questions about the universe.

As I got older I stopped thinking much about space, and left it to the boys to read science fiction and watch *Star Trek*. But more recently, whenever I'm away from city lights, I've started looking more at the stars, and re-learning the constellations. My husband developed an obsession with the spacecraft which were launched in the 70s. It was in the news that Voyager 1 is now reaching the outer edges of our solar system, after travelling for 34 years and covering over 17 billion kilometres. As it heads for interstellar space, it will apparently take at least 40,000 years to reach the next star, in the constellation Ursa Minor. That's how much space is out there, between our Sun and the next little pinprick of light, just one of billions and billions of stars stretching throughout the universe.

You can hardly begin to imagine the vastness of this space! It might feel overwhelming, but I find it strangely comforting. I tend to think I have to look after everything, or the world will fall apart. When I remember this limitless space, it seems to put it all in perspective. If I notice I'm feeling overwhelmed, I look up and connect with the sky, and the feeling of space stretching outward, and it feels like a fresh breeze comes into the situation.

 You can have a sense of stillness and equanimity within the chaos of everyday life. Remembering the vastness of the sky or the stability of a mountain can help you to embody these qualities.

22. Where next?

As you come to the end of this book, hopefully you have a taste of what mindfulness is about. It might be a raisin-sized nibble, or a few juicy mouthfuls, depending especially on how much you've been trying out the exercises. So what do you think? Do you feel any inspiration to pursue this further?

Intention: going forward

- Take a few moments to feel grounded in your body and bring awareness to your breath.

- Reflect on your experience of reading this book and doing some of the practices. Is there anything you have discovered for yourself that you would like to remember? Write down your thoughts, either here or in a notebook. Something you discovered from exploring/ practising mindfulness so far:

_____

_____

_____

- Bring your mind back to your original intention. Why were you interested in mindfulness? If you wrote something down in Chapter 3, you could look at this again. Is this still your intention going forward, or has anything changed? Would you like to develop your mindfulness practice further, and if so why? Your intention going forward:

_____

_____

Reasons why you'd like to practise mindfulness (or if not, reasons why not):

_____

_____

Finding a teacher

Books can be a good introduction, but mindfulness is really an oral tradition. The practices we do have been passed from teacher to student for centuries, with each new teacher adding the flavour of their own insight. If you're serious about mindfulness, it's important to have the support of a live teacher. This is someone who can share their own understanding of the practices, and can help you to articulate your own experience and to see more clearly what you can learn from it. They should be a person who has a regular mindfulness practice themselves, and who has been trained to support other people's practice through friendly questioning, listening and responding.

You are not alone

While mindfulness practices do encourage us to be alone with ourselves, it's also extremely helpful to practise with other people. Sitting in silence in a group is surprisingly powerful. And you can learn a lot from discussing your practice with others. Sometimes they will say something which resonates; sometimes they will come from a completely different angle to you. In either case this can help to clarify your own experience. You can find fellow practitioners by joining a course, or by connecting with a local meditation centre.

The eight-week courses known as MBSR (Mindfulness-Based Stress Reduction) and MBCT (Mindfulness-Based Cognitive Therapy) are widely recognized by the international medical community, and research shows their many benefits for health and wellbeing (see Chapter 3). A structured course like this can help you to embed the practices in your daily life, with the support of a teacher and a group. MBSR and MBCT are very closely related, and participants don't usually experience a big difference between the two – you may find the choice is made by which one is offered near you. If you have an ongoing mental health issue such as depression or anxiety disorder, then MBCT can offer you more specific help working with negative thought patterns, and courses are run by clinical psychologists trained to work with depression. Mindfulness teachers normally offer an assessment process before you sign up, so you can discuss with them whether their course is the right one for you at this time in your life.

Another way to deepen your experience is to find a local meditation centre or group. Many Buddhist centres offer regular meditation sessions where you can practise with other people, without having to sign up to any beliefs or become a Buddhist. There are other faith-based organizations such as Christian churches which run meditation sessions, as well as secular groups of mindfulness practitioners. You'll need to research the organization to avoid anything cultish, and be discriminating about the kind of meditation that is practised. Some forms of meditation may be more about going off into an altered state, or serving a particular 'higher purpose'. Without denigrating these traditions, if it's *mindfulness* you're interested in, ask yourself if the meditation supports the purposes of mindfulness discussed in this book. Does it help you to be more aware and present? More embodied? More accepting of yourself and others?

If you don't have a course or group near you, another option is to go for a big feast of mindfulness all in one go, by travelling to a retreat centre. Every Western country has places where you can learn to meditate for a weekend, a week or more, often in beautiful countryside settings. Some retreats are relaxed and sociable; others take a more monastic approach, with early rising and a rule of silence. This can be a wonderful opportunity to discover what happens when you let your mind and body really slow down and settle in one place.

Tessa

For me, one of the best things about practising mindfulness has been the connection with other people. When you're meditating you really need to be with other people who find it normal to sit on their bum in silence for hours at a time. When I first started meditating, all my friends were in their 20s and 30s working in the media. I came to the meditation centre and there were people of all ages and backgrounds – nurses, actors, lecturers, gardeners, builders, policemen, business people and students. It felt refreshing. I was very wary of anything cultish, but I relaxed when no one seemed to be interested in converting me to anything.

When you spend time meditating, people seem to soften up and become more open and relaxed with each other. I used to size people up to see whether they were a good advert for meditation. Then at some point it clicked that there wasn't a type of person they were going to become. They were each just more and more themselves. Jim was very Jim, Isaac was unique in his Isaac-ness and Debbie was increasingly Debbie. That was a great relief – that I could relax into being Tessa.

Inspiration

We're bombarded daily by images and words encouraging us to be mindless – free newspapers with gossip about celebrities we'll forget five minutes later, billboards which steal our attention with their slogans, and TV which can leave us hypnotized on the sofa. How do you escape from all that to make space for meditation?

You can counteract this by seeking out books, audio and video which inspire you to meditate and remind you why you practise. There are books which offer practical guidance, including a few which will take you step-by-step through an eight-week mindfulness course. You can also take inspiration from great meditation masters and teachers from different traditions, each with their own way of putting things which can bring a fresh viewpoint – as you read, suddenly something goes *ping* inside you. Poetry, music and visual art can also remind us to be mindful. Artists often capture the essence of the present moment – its simplicity and magic.

Your own practice

It's lovely to read and talk about mindfulness, and you may think 'Yes that's great, I sign up to that!' However, there's no substitute for actually doing the practice! Words can only point in the vague general direction – you have to experience it in your own body and being. Think of your practice as a small plant you've been given to look after. You need to water it daily rather than letting it dry out for ages, and then hoping to revive it with a drenching. If you keep watering you may find it surprises you by producing unexpected fruit or a vivid blossom.

- **Time**
  See if you can find a regular time of day which works for you. Some people like the freshness of the morning; others feel more relaxed in the evening. Some people even manage to find a quiet meeting room at work in their lunch break. Experiment in your own life, and then see if you can create a habit.

- **Place**
  Create a physical space for your practice. It may just be a small corner of your room, but see if you can find a place to meditate which isn't full of clutter or dirty laundry. You could have a plant or picture to inspire you. See if you can create a little space which calls invitingly for you to come and practise your mindfulness.

- **Keeping a record**

  Keep a diary of your practice. Just making a quick note each day can help you to see more clearly when you are keeping up your practice or letting things drop off, and what effect that has on your state of mind.

- **Any little helps**

  It's better to practise for 10 minutes a day than for a marathon session once in a blue moon. Even 2 or 3 minutes of practice can help you reconnect with the sense of being present.

 Aaron

I've found that for me it helps to get up in the morning and do it first thing. I have breakfast, brush my teeth, have my shower – feel comfortable with myself. Then I sit down and meditate. One of my teachers said that for him not meditating is like not brushing his teeth. After a while I do feel like my brain has bad breath if I haven't been meditating. And it doesn't feel good to go out with a messy mind, to go out there and meet other people with my bad breath brain.

Isaac

It was a great discovery for me, finding out that it was easier for me to do at night, just before I went to sleep. Rather than my head hitting the pillow and having thoughts running right the way through, I found the thoughts would already have exhausted themselves if I meditated first.

There've been moments when things in my life were getting heavy, where I've felt there was just so much I had to get a grip of, I didn't have the time to meditate. Actually, it's these times when you really need to meditate. Those 5 minutes – if I'm able to do it in the maelstrom – make all the difference. There's a part of me that thinks 'If I meditate now I'm not going to do it properly, am I? I'm all over the place.' The point is just to 'come as you are'. You don't have to be in a particular state for you to start – you can just do it at that point.

Where next?

Would you like to explore mindfulness further? If so, take a few moments to reflect about practical next steps. Will you find a course? Read another book? Set aside time for daily practice? What sort of challenges do you think may come up, and how could you work with them? Write down your thoughts here or in a notebook.

Your next steps (e.g. course, book, meditation centre, regular practice):

_____

_____

A formal practice you will try to do regularly for the next month (e.g. mindful breathing, body scan, mindful movement):

_____

_____

When you will practise (e.g. morning, lunchtime, evening, whenever you can):

_____

An informal practice you will try to do regularly for the next month (e.g. mindful tooth brushing, pausing, mindful walking to work):

_____

_____

What are likely to be your obstacles or challenges to practising?

_____

_____

What would help you with these challenges?

_____

_____

One word or phrase which will help you remember why you'd like to practise mindfulness:

_____

_____

As things are now

Quick now, here, now, always–

T. S. Eliot

It could be easy to think of mindfulness as a self-improvement plan. Most of us tend to think there's something wrong with us, or our lives, and one day we will fix it. But mindfulness

194

is not about striving to be better. We can let go of this idea that things need to be different from how they are right now. Yes, it helps if we can put a bit of energy and thought into making space for mindfulness practices. But we're creating space within which we can stop doing and striving, and simply be here, just as we are.

You could feel overwhelmed by life's busyness and give yourself a hard time for not being more mindful as you go through your day. But none of us are walking around being mindful and awake at every moment. It's a constant movement in and out of awareness: opening, closing and opening again to the vividness of our experience.

Each time you are 'mindless' is another opportunity to be mindful again – each time you can enjoy your rediscovery of the present moment. 'Oh look!' Here we are again – back in the 'now' at any moment. You're off in a long boring conversation in your head, and suddenly you're brought back by the bright green of a tree, the hot water of the shower, the taste of a strawberry. The more you were off in the clouds, the more you can take delight in coming back.

He who binds to himself a joy
Does the wingèd life destroy
But he who kisses the joy as it flies
Lives in eternity's sun rise.

William Blake

We can't hold anything still. The shower will be over, the strawberry will be eaten, and a new 'now' will come along to take its place. Sometimes the now is difficult and challenging, sometimes surprising and magical. May your mindfulness practice help you to be at ease with now, whatever it may bring!

List of practices

We have worked with a lot of exercises in this book. Many of them are variations on a theme – starting with a basic practice like mindful breathing, and revisiting it with a different focus or emphasis. Once you've got a flavour of these different possibilities, it would be good to choose just one or two practices to get familiar with and explore in more depth.

Sitting meditation
- Mindfulness of breathing (p. 39)
- Mindfulness of breathing: being inquisitive (p. 43)
- Mindfulness of sounds (p. 97)
- Mindfulness of breathing: labelling thoughts (p. 117)
- Mindfulness of breath, sounds and thoughts (p. 120)
- Working with challenges (p. 146)
- Loving kindness meditation (p. 152)
- Meditation: mountain (p. 179)
- Meditation: sky (p. 181)

Mindfulness of body
- Body in stress (p. 53)
- Feeling your fingers (p. 55)
- Feet and legs (p. 57)
- Full body scan (p. 62)
- Words and sensations (p. 105)

Mindfulness in daily life

Further resources

Books

Mindfulness in depth
These books will help you to go further into mindfulness practice as it is taught in the MBSR and MBCT programmes.

Full Catastrophe Living: Using the Wisdom of Your Body and Mind to Face Stress, Pain and Illness by Jon Kabat-Zinn (Delta, 1990)
This influential book presenting mindfulness and its benefits for health and wellbeing is by Jon Kabat-Zinn, creator of the Mindfulness-Based Stress Reduction programme.

Mindfulness: A Practical Guide to Finding Peace in a Frantic World by Mark Williams and Danny Penman (Piatkus, 2011)
Professor Mark Williams, one of the founders of Mindfulness-Based Cognitive Therapy, takes you through an eight-week mindfulness programme, including a CD for guided practice.

Mindfulness: How to Live Well by Paying Attention by Ed Halliwell (Hay House, 2015)
A clear and accessible guide which can be used as a nine-week training manual.

Mindfulness for Health: A practical guide to relieving pain, reducing stress and restoring wellbeing by Vidyamala Burch and Danny Penman (Piatkus, 2013)
Practices to relieve chronic pain and the stress of illness, developed by Vidyamala Burch to help cope with her own spinal injury.

Mindfulness-Based Cognitive Therapy by Rebecca Crane (Routledge, 2009)
This book provides a clear and thorough outline of the key theoretical and practical features of MBCT, mainly for use by mindfulness teachers and therapists.

Mindfulness–Based Cognitive Therapy for Depression. A New Approach to Preventing Relapse by Zindel V. Segal, J. Mark G. Williams and John D. Teasdale (Guilford Press, 2002)
This seminal work on MBCT is mainly for use by mindfulness teachers and therapists. For a book written more for the general public see the next title by the same authors and Jon Kabat-Zinn.

The Mindful Way through Depression by Mark Williams, John Teasdale, Zindel V. Segal and Jon Kabat-Zinn (Guilford Press, 2007)
A guide to mindfulness, including CD, for anyone who has struggled with depression, written by the founders of Mindfulness-Based Cognitive Therapy.

Mindfulness, meditation and inspiration

These are guides to mindfulness, meditation and life by writers and teachers from a range of backgrounds and traditions.

Get Some Headspace by Andy Puddicombe (Hodder & Stoughton, 2011)
A practical guide to meditation by a clinical consultant and former Buddhist monk who suggests that ten minutes a day of practice can have life-changing effects.

In Praise of Slow by Carl Honoré (Orion, 2005)
Journalist Carl Honoré explores the rise of slow movements in food, workplaces, medicine, urban planning and other areas – challenging the idea that faster is always better.

The Mindful Manifesto: How Doing Less And Noticing More Can Help Us Thrive In A Stressed-Out World by Dr Jonty Heaversedge and Ed Halliwell (2nd edn, Hay House, 2012)
An inspiring overview of mindfulness research and practice, offering a vision of a more mindful society.

The Mindful Workplace: Developing Resilient Individuals and Resonant Organizations with MBSR by Michael Chaskalson (Wiley-Blackwell, 2011)

One of the UK's leading proponents of mindfulness in the workplace offers a practical and theoretical guide to mindfulness in organizational settings.

The Miracle of Mindfulness, by Thich Nhat Hanh (Rider, 1991)
One of the West's most popular Buddhist teachers, the Vietnamese monk Thich Nhat Hanh, encourages meditation practice through gentle anecdotes and exercises.

The Power of Now: A Guide to Spiritual Enlightenment by Eckhart Tolle (New World Library, 1999)
This best-selling book is too 'New Age' for some, but many readers have been inspired by Tolle's vision of how to become more fully present.

Sane New World: Taming the Mind by Ruby Wax (Hodder & Stoughton, 2013)
Comedian Ruby Wax has her own experience of depression and now a Masters from Oxford in Mindfulness-based Cognitive Therapy. She presents an honest, funny manual for rewiring our brains and living more calmly.

Seeking the Heart of Wisdom: The Path of Insight Meditation by Jack Goldstein and Jack Kornfield (Shambhala, 1987)
An introduction to Insight Meditation, which brings the teachings of Theravada Buddhism (rooted especially in Southeast Asia) into an accessible context for Westerners.

Shambhala: The Sacred Path of the Warrior by Chögyam Trungpa (Shambhala, 2007)
The Tibetan meditation master Chögyam Trungpa teaches how to live a life of fearlessness and goodness based on the Shambhala teachings, named for a legendary enlightened kingdom.

Taking the Leap: Freeing Ourselves from Old Habits and Fears by Pema Chödrön (Shambhala, 2010)
American Buddhist nun Pema Chödrön teaches how to break free of destructive patterns in our life by learning to stay present and open.

Turning the Mind into an Ally by Sakyong Mipham (Riverhead, 2004)
Sakyong Mipham writes with clarity about how to strengthen our minds and bring peace to our lives through the practice of meditation.

When Things Fall Apart: Heart Advice for Difficult Times by Pema Chödrön (Shambhala, 2000)
Pema Chödrön teaches with her usual humour and compassion on how to work with painful situations and emotions.

Wherever You Go, There You Are. Mindfulness Meditation for Everyday Life by Jon Kabat-Zinn (Piatkus, 1994)
This book by Jon Kabat-Zinn is less about medicine and health (compared with his earlier *Full Catastrophe Living*) and more of a personal and poetic guide to the practice of mindfulness.

APPs
Buddify
buddhify.com
This beautifully designed UK app brings mindfulness into daily life, with guided meditations to use when walking, eating, waking up, waiting around, and so on.

Headspace
getsomeheadspace.com
'The world's first gym membership for the mind', with guided meditations from British former Buddhist monk Andy Puddicombe. The free programme offers ten days of ten-minute meditation practices, and animations to support your understanding. After the trial period you can pay for a wide range of further content.

Insight Timer
insighttimer.com
A free app to time your meditation session, with sounds of various gongs or singing bowls. You can also log your practice or choose to connect with others meditating worldwide.

The Mindfulness App
mindapps.se
This American app comes with guided meditation practices between three and 30 minutes, a silent meditation option and body-scan practice.

Whil

www.whil.com

An extensive range of meditation and yoga sessions of varying lengths led by American and global teachers.

Websites

Be Mindful

www.bemindful.co.uk

The Mental Health Foundation hosts a site with a wealth of information about mindfulness, including a directory where you can find current courses offered by teachers across the UK.

Be Mindful Online

www.bemindfulonline.com

A four-week online course run by the Mental Health Foundation and presented by Tessa Watt and Ed Halliwell. It features video lessons, guided audio, and interactive exercises.

Being Mindful

www.beingmindful.co.uk

The author is co-director of this small London-based organization which offers MBSR courses, sessions for workplaces, and mindfulness coaching.

The Center for Mindfulness in Medicine, Health Care and Society
www.umassmed.edu/cfm/
This organization based at the University of Massachusetts Medical School grew out of Jon Kabat-Zinn's pioneering Stress Reduction Clinic, and is the home of MBSR. On the website you can find mindfulness programmes in North America, and information on the Center's research into mindfulness in healthcare.

The Centre for Mindfulness Research and Practice
www.bangor.ac.uk/mindfulness
Based at Bangor University in Wales, this centre is a leading provider of professional mindfulness training. It also offers public courses including a distance learning programme, in which you can follow an eight-week course supported by weekly phone calls with a teacher. The website also has guided mindfulness meditation CDs for sale.

Gaia House
www.gaiahouse.co.uk
This site gives information on Insight Meditation retreats in the Buddhist tradition, based in Devon, UK.

Mindful
www.mindful.org
This lively website features stories and commentary about mindfulness and 'mindful society'. There is news of projects

in schools, hospitals, offices, campuses, prisons and so on, as well as updates on scientific research, and articles on practical subjects like mindful parenting.

Mindfulness-Based Cognitive Therapy (UK)
www.mbct.co.uk
The official UK website of MBCT contains information and links to other resources.

Mindfulness Meditation Practice CDs and Tapes
www.mindfulnesstapes.com
Here you can order CDs and tapes recorded by MBSR founder Jon Kabat-Zinn.

American Mindfulness Research Association
goamra.org
A resource providing information on the scientific study of mindfulness, including publications, measurement tools and research centres.

Oxford Mindfulness Centre
www.oxfordmindfulness.org
The Oxford Mindfulness Centre is a charity working to research and promote the therapeutic use of mindfulness. On this site you can download academic papers on the use of mindfulness for working with specific mental health challenges such as bipolar disorder, suicidal behaviour and eating disorders.

Shambhala

www.shambhala.org

An international network of meditation centres rooted in the Buddhist tradition but offering meditation evenings and courses open to all, in over 170 locations worldwide.

Acknowledgements

I'd like to thank all my teachers and friends on this journey into mindfulness and meditation over the years. In particular, enormous thanks go to my mindfulness mentor Cindy Cooper for her generosity and wisdom in reading and commenting on my drafts of this book. Thank you Cindy for all your support and encouragement!

I'd like to express my deep appreciation to my Being Mindful colleague Debbie Johnson for her friendship, partnership and 'heartfulness'. Special thanks to Ed Halliwell for sharing his inspiration to make the benefits of meditation more widely known. I'm grateful to my wonderful Slow Down colleague Deepa Patel for always reminding me what it means to embody the practice in our lives. Thank you to the many dedicated teachers at Shambhala, especially my meditation instructor Jim O'Neill, and of course our inspiring teacher Sakyong Mipham Rinpoche.

Many thanks to Duncan Heath at Icon Books for inviting me to write this book, and to Harry Scoble for his careful and sensitive editing. I'm grateful to Professor Mark Williams for his advice, and my friend Anna Janmaat for her kind feedback. Thank you to the people who have shared their own experiences of mindfulness for this book: Marion, Sarah, Isaac, Anthony, Debbie and Aaron. I'd also like to thank the participants in my courses at Being Mindful, for bringing their fresh experience to the practices and always teaching me something new.

I'm grateful to my brother Nicholas Watt for introducing me to yoga, and my father Frank Watt for encouraging me to write from an early age. Thanks to Frank and Emily for sharing Three Ponds Farm, my favourite place for meditation practice and mindful swimming.

Finally my huge thanks to my family Richard, Katrina and Tanya Woolley for giving me the space and time for practice, and for all their love and support.

May you be safe, may you be happy, may you be free from suffering, may you be at ease.

Index

215

HPL

217